Jan., 1969

THE POLITICAL BELIEFS
OF AMERICANS

A STUDY OF PUBLIC OPINION

by LLOYD A. FREE *and* HADLEY CANTRIL

A CLARION BOOK
PUBLISHED BY SIMON AND SCHUSTER

99115

To our sons, Tad and Peter

Contents

Contents

List of Tables

List of Tables

TABLES IN APPENDICES

Acknowledgments

To allow the reader to apportion the blame for this book, the co-author, my associate Hadley Cantril, insists that I confess to being primarily guilty for most of it. On the other hand, I insist on making it clear that his is the responsibility especially for the last chapter, the most important and difficult to formulate.

But guilt, at least by association, must be assigned more broadly. First, to those who pioneered in the development of public opinion survey techniques, such as George Gallup, Elmo Roper, Archibald Crossley, and, indeed, the co-author himself. Secondly, to those who have charted the way in studies of political attitudes and behavior, such as Paul Lazarsfeld, Bernard Berelson, and Angus Campbell.

The level of analysis in most of this study has necessarily been determined by the fact that I am a pollster and a political analyst, not a psychologist or a sociologist. I am also not a statistician and have not used in this book such formal statistical techniques as significance tests and confidence intervals. Since all the basic data are presented, those persons who are skilled and interested enough to apply these techniques can do so at their pleasure. In selecting the information to be gathered and in analyzing and presenting it, I have had primarily in mind the politician and the student of practical politics. Accordingly, I have not attempted to trace causation in depth.

Needless to say, I am indebted to a number of people for help. To the co-author's son, Dr. Albert H. Cantril, Jr., who aided in drawing up the questionnaires. To several members of the Gallup Poll organization, which handled the interviewing, and especially Charles Roll, Jr., who not only assisted in the formulation of the study but served as the principal liaison in seeing the field work through to completion. My son, Peter, also worked during one summer vacation gathering material for me. The tabulating, which yielded over five thousand statistical tables out of the computers, was handled by Market Probe International, under the able direction of George Biro. Both Cantril and Roll made suggestions which improved the final manuscript. I am grateful to Alice Anne Navin for her editorial assistance.

Then, I am grateful to several individuals and organizations whose polling data I have cited in supplementation of our own: to the National Opinion Research Center, to *Fortune* magazine, to the Survey Research Center of the University of Michigan, and to the Opinion Research Corporation; but, above all, to Dr. George Gallup and Mr. Louis Harris, whose material I have drawn upon heavily.

Finally, I am grateful to my wife, Elsbeth, who put up with me with great patience during the irritable days and sleepless nights that were the cost of writing this book.

Lloyd A. Free

Institute for International
  Social Research
Princeton, New Jersey
May 10, 1967

THE POLITICAL BELIEFS
OF AMERICANS

I

The Study and Its Setting

Rarely have the two dominant schools of political thought in the United States confronted each other as dramatically as they did in the Presidential campaign of 1964, in the persons of Lyndon Johnson and Barry Goldwater. If the campaign often seemed to generate more heat than light, as campaigns have a habit of doing, nevertheless it served to arouse American political consciousness. The time therefore seemed especially propitious for a study of American political beliefs, values, and attitudes as regards not only national but international issues. For this reason and also because we hoped thereby to provide a basis for analyzing the implications of the coming election, we set out during the campaign to chart the mainstream of American political opinion.

Differentiating "Liberals" and "Conservatives"

The heart of this study is the survey we carried out in the fall of 1964 through the interviewing facilities of the Gallup Poll.* From time to time we also refer to data from several

* The bulk of the data stems from two regular Gallup samples of around sixteen hundred cases each, representing national cross sections

special, more limited surveys conducted in our behalf by
the Gallup organization, both before and after the main
survey, and also to the regular, published releases of various
polling outfits, particularly those of George Gallup and
Louis Harris.

The results on questions dealing with foreign affairs are
discussed primarily in Chapter VI on "International Outlooks" and require no comment here. In the case of questions on domestic matters, however, a brief word of background is necessary about our use of the terms "liberal"
and "conservative," if only to clarify them for people feeling
the way a sixty-year-old California real estate man we interviewed did, who said:

> I would consider myself a conservative, perhaps even an
> ultra-conservative, if there is such a thing. But that's strange,
> too. You know, I have gone through school and worked
> here, just an ordinary fellow trying to live the way my
> parents taught me to and the way I learned in school, and
> now I find myself belonging to a group which is considered
> sort of right-wing extremist. But *we* haven't changed. It's
> just that everything around us is moving to the left.

Probably the meaning of few words in English or any
other language has come around full circle to the same extent as "liberal" and "liberalism." [1] According to the older
definition, the term "liberalism," of course, had to do
primarily with the protection of the individual against en-

of the adult population. (See Appendix A, pp. 185 f., for the design of
the samples.) Certain key questions were asked in both of the surveys,
so that the total number of Americans interviewed reached 3,175. Less
important questions were put to only one or the other of the two
sample populations, permitting us to cover a wider range of problems.
The questions asked and the responses to them are reproduced in
Appendix B, pp. 187 ff., with an indication of the number of cases upon
which the results on each question were based.

croachment by the state; its essence was individualism. Self-reliance, individual initiative, and private enterprise were unqualifiedly good. Government was the enemy to be distrusted and held in check. At the political level, the assumptions of old-style liberalism dictated a system of checks and balances and a division of power between the states and the Federal Government, with the latter having distinctly limited powers and all matters closest to the lives of the citizens being reserved to the states.

At the economic and social level, liberalism as then defined was closely linked to laissez-faire. Private property was sanctified. Private enterprise was looked upon not only as a direct expression of economic freedom but as important also in facilitating political liberty. Particularly after the Civil War, the prevailing theories of social Darwinism held that competition, unimpeded by government, assured the survival of the fittest. Poverty was considered the result of inherent inferiorities. State intervention, by inhibiting the development of individual initiative and responsibility, was seen as stultifying the development of character and protecting the lazy, the inefficient, and the shiftless. These doctrines of "liberalism" (old style), widely propagated by the stories of Horatio Alger, are what we mean by the traditional American ideology.

The main point to be made here is that in the seventeenth and eighteenth centuries, when the doctrines of "liberalism" described above were first advanced, they were devised and resorted to by "liberals" in the sense of innovators: men like Locke, Montesquieu, and Adam Smith, who were attacking the status quo, particularly (1) the domination of government by the aristocratic class and (2) the "mercantile system" under which that government stifled the rising industrial class. Their philosophy was designed to rationalize change, and hence was "liberal" in character.

By the middle of the nineteenth century, however, the doctrines of liberalism, as further developed by such men as Spencer and Sumner, were being used for exactly the opposite purpose: namely, by "conservatives" to defend a new status quo. By this time, particularly after the Civil War, the business class was in the saddle and was fearful that, with the extension of suffrage, governments would prove too sensitive to the needs of the people and adopt dangerous working-class reforms. Thus, while the doctrines of liberalism remained essentially the same, they were taken over from the liberals by the conservatives, and the term "liberalism" came to mean resistance to change and the rationalization of the status quo. For this reason we refer in this book to the traditional American ideology as conservative rather than liberal, despite its origins.

In the twentieth century, however, a new liberalism in the present-day sense of the term was gradually emerging in some of the states and was heralded at the Federal level by the progressive regimes of Theodore Roosevelt and Woodrow Wilson. As a practical matter, the new style liberals increasingly recognized the need for governmental action to protect the underprivileged. They favored strengthening the powers of government in the interest of the public welfare, with particular attention to social amelioration. They supported compulsory education, unemployment and old-age insurance, minimum wages, and the like as enlargements of, not restrictions on, individual liberty. Earlier, resort to government was condoned to advance economic development; now, the idea was to use government to promote social justice. This new liberalism accomplished an enduring breakthrough with the election of Franklin D. Roosevelt to the Presidency in 1932.

However, neither Roosevelt nor those who followed him ever evolved a coherent philosophy of liberalism (new style) to rationalize the programs they supported. The approach has tended to be based on "problem solving" in the light of social conscience, rather than on any ideological premise.[2] In our survey, therefore, while we were able to ask questions about the traditional American ideology—"liberalism" old style—we were unable to unearth a sufficiently coherent body of ideological doctrine commonly accepted by the public to ask questions about "liberalism" new style. We had to probe public attitudes about practical applications of the new liberalism rather than about the new liberalism in theory.

Whatever the definitions of "liberal" and "conservative" from the historical point of view, it appears to us that, practically speaking, one of the best ways to differentiate liberals from conservatives in this country under present conditions is to test attitudes toward new uses of the power and resources of the Federal Government as the means to accomplish domestic social objectives. The general disposition of the liberals is to approve of such use, of the conservatives to disapprove. There are, no doubt, other connotations for these terms, having to do, for example, with international affairs and such special fields as civil rights. But, as we see it, more than anything else the core of the difference between liberals and conservatives in their attitudes, words, and political behavior is this underlying disagreement about the use of Federal power and resources for social ends. It is in this limited, primary sense that we shall use the terms "liberal" and "conservative" in this book.

Growth of the Federal Government

As will become apparent below, the majority of Americans remain conservative at the ideological level in the sense that they continue to accept the traditional American ideology, which advocates the curbing of Federal power. Yet, at the practical level of Governmental operations, there has been an apparently inexorable trend in liberal directions in the United States since the days of the New Deal. This has been reflected in the increased size of the Federal Government and the Government's willingness to use its power for social purposes. In a crude way, this trend can be gauged by the increase in Federal expenditures. At the beginning of the 1930's, before the New Deal, the total Government outlays of the Hoover Administration came to about $3.5 billion per year. In fiscal 1966, excluding the costs of the Vietnam war, which must be considered extraordinary, the Federal Government (on a consolidated cash basis, including trust fund expenditures) paid out over $136 billion—almost thirty-nine times the earlier figure. Of course, allowances must be made for the great increase in population in the intervening years and for the decrease in the value of the dollar, but the bald, unadjusted figures give a vivid idea of what has happened in the past few decades.

By now, approximately one out of every five of those who work in this country are paid by Federal funds, either directly in the form of wages and salaries or indirectly through grants and contracts. Similarly, the Federal Government has become such a big buyer that it consumes nearly one-fifth of everything produced in the United States. This is only one of a number of factors that give the Government such enormous leverage over the American economy.

There is now, obviously, a greater degree of Governmental involvement in the nation's economy than ever before in peace time. According to pollster Louis Harris, this involvement is generally approved by the public: "People believe that the Federal Government is a key element in keeping the economy balanced through its taxing, spending and regulatory powers. In a broad sense, then, it is fair to conclude that the underlying notion of Keynesian eco-

nomics—of Government seeking to maintain stability and
steady growth of an essentially privately run system—meets
with general approval." [3]

One of the most pronounced developments antithetical
to old-style liberal doctrines is the degree to which the national government has become involved in aid to the public.
Estimates vary, but there is no doubt that the United States
Government is currently spending many billions of dollars
a year on a galaxy of welfare programs. As the Republican
Minority Leader in the House of Representatives recently
claimed: "There are now over 400 Federal aid appropria-
tions for 170 separate aid programs administered by a total
of 21 Federal departments and agencies, 150 Washington
bureaus and 400 regional offices, each with its own way of
passing out Federal tax dollars." *Time* magazine, in an
essay entitled "What Big Daddy, Alias Uncle Sam, Will Do
for You," had the following to say (November 5, 1965):

> In the remote past, America's prevailing political philos-
> ophy held with Lincoln that government should do for the
> people only those necessary things that the people could
> not do for themselves. That notion now seems hopelessly
> quaint. Today's generations take it for granted that the
> U.S. Government is simply bursting with good deeds to per-
> form for the individual, whether strictly necessary or not.
> . . . How Uncle Sam turned into Big Daddy is delineated
> in *The Encyclopedia of U.S. Government Benefits*. . . . To
> move through its 1,011 pages is to have one's eyes opened to
> a wonderland of federal paternalism that stretches from
> cradle to grave . . .

Whether or not the United States has already become a
welfare state depends upon varying definitions; that it has
been moving in that direction, no one can deny. But what
do the America people think of this trend against the background of traditional American ideology? The press re-

ported, in the words of *The New York Times* of January 2, 1966, that President Johnson believes "the developments of 1965, coupled with the election of 1964, show that the old argument over the 'welfare state' has been resolved in favor of Federal action." But is this really the case? Has the old argument actually been resolved? In the following chapters, we will attempt to answer these questions with findings from our study.

II

Government Programs and Governmental Power

Popular Support for Government Programs

President Johnson announced in a speech he made on October 16, 1966:

> Our domestic policy here at home is to find jobs for our men at good wages, education for our children, a roof over their heads . . . adequate food for their bodies, and health for their families.

An Iowa dairy worker, asked where the U.S. will be ten years from now, said:

> It depends on the election. It will be fine if it goes Democratic: better working conditions, care for the elderly, better social security, medicare, help for the poor.

An automobile worker in Michigan remarked:

> It might sound funny, but they've got a good thing over in Sweden. You're protected from the cradle to the grave. Not that I'm socialist or anything like that, but it would be a good thing for the U.S. to follow.

A majority of the American people have been "liberal" in the sense of favoring Government programs to accomplish

9

social objectives at least since the days of the New Deal, which happened to be the time when scientific public opinion polling first began. Three decades ago:

Eight out of ten members of the public favored "an amendment to the Constitution prohibiting child labor." (Gallup: March 28, 1936.)

Six out of ten thought "the Federal Government ought to set a limit on the number of hours employees should work in each business and industry." (Gallup: July 26, 1937.)

Seven out of ten approved Government regulation of the stock exchanges. (Gallup: October 17, 1937.)

Six out of ten approved minimum wage regulations. (Gallup: June 6, 1937.)

Nine out of ten were in favor "of Government Old Age Pensions for needy persons." (Gallup: January 12, 1936.)

Seven out of ten thought "the Federal Government should give money to the states to help local schools." (Gallup: March 26, 1938.)

Eight out of ten felt the Federal Government should "provide free medical care for those unable to pay." (Gallup: June 14, 1937.)

Three-fourths believed "the government should see to it that any man who wants to work has a job." (*Fortune:* July 1935.)

Seven out of ten thought "it is the government's responsibility to pay the living expenses of needy people who are out of work." (Gallup: April 5, 1939.)

In the mid-1960's, this general trend of thought still continued. A special survey done for us by the Gallup organization in December 1963 and January 1964 demonstrated that three-fourths of the public favored Federal aid "to depressed areas, that is, where unemployment has been high over a long period," either at the present or an increased level; and close to two-thirds thought the Federal Government should be spending more for the construction of nursing homes for the elderly. A regular Gallup survey showed that a majority believed the Federal Government should use its powers to raise the minimum wage above the then current level of $1.25 per hour (September 29, 1965). Seven out of ten were willing to have more of their tax money spent for the treatment of mental illness, nearly the same proportion for unemployment compensation, and almost six out of ten for low-interest Federal housing loans (Harris: *Newsweek,* January 11, 1965). Seven out of ten endorsed the anti-poverty program (Harris: *Newsweek,* October 19, 1964). One-half favored a Federal plan such as Medicare to cover, not just the elderly, but all members of the family, with only four in ten opposing (Harris: January 23, 1967).

Even in the aftermath of the 1966 elections, which were widely interpreted as signalling a trend toward conservatism, a special survey conducted for us by the Gallup organization during the first half of February 1967 showed that majorities still favored various key programs of the Johnson Administration, including the highly controversial Community Action program.

> QUESTION: Under the Community Action program, the Federal Government makes grants to city governments and private organizations so that they can carry out local projects with the idea of combatting poverty. Do you think spending by the Federal Government for this purpose should be kept at least at the present level, or reduced, or ended altogether?

Present level or increased	54%
Reduced	25
Ended altogether	10
Don't know	11
	100%

QUESTION: Under the Head Start program, the Federal Government finances schooling for very young children from poor families even before they reach the usual school age with the idea of improving their educational opportunities. Do you think spending by the Federal Government for this purpose should be kept at least at the present level, or reduced, or ended altogether?

Present level or increased	67%
Reduced	10
Ended altogether	16
Don't know	7
	100%

QUESTION: As part of the anti-poverty program, the Federal Government is providing funds for retraining poorly educated people so they can get jobs. Do you think spending by the Federal Government for this purpose should be kept at least at the present level, or reduced, or ended altogether?

Present level or increased	75%
Reduced	13
Ended altogether	8
Don't know	4
	100%

Also after the 1966 elections, Harris found that the predominant opinion was actually in favor of an expansion of Federal programs having to do with curbing air and water pollution and providing scholarships for needy college students; and substantial majorities opposed any reduction in current programs involving Federal grants for low income housing, for highway construction, and for welfare and relief payments (April 3, 1967).

Thus, from the New Deal days to the present, there has been a substantial, general consensus among Americans that at the operational level of Government programs, the Federal Government should act to meet public needs. This conclusion clearly emerges from the results obtained in our own survey in the fall of 1964, when samples of Americans were questioned on six crucial areas involving the utilization of Federal power and resources for the public welfare: education, Medicare, public housing, urban renewal, unemployment, and poverty. Here are the questions asked and the results obtained:

QUESTION: A broad general program of Federal aid to education is under consideration, which would include Federal grants to help pay teachers' salaries. Would you be for or against such a program?

For	62%
Against	28
Don't know	10
	100%

QUESTION: Congress has been considering a compulsory medical insurance program covering hospital and nursing home care for the elderly. This Medicare program would be financed out of increased social security taxes. In general, do you approve or disapprove of this program?

Approve	63%
Disapprove	30
Don't know	7
	100%

QUESTION: Under the Federal housing program, the Federal Government is making grants to help build low-rent public housing. Do you think government spending for this purpose should be kept at least at the present level, or reduced, or ended altogether?

Present level or increased	63%
Reduced	12
Ended altogether	10
Don't know	15
	100%

QUESTION: Under the urban renewal program, the Federal Government is making grants to help rebuild run-down sections of our cities. Do you think government spending for this purpose should be kept at least at the present level, or reduced, or ended altogether?

Present level or increased	67%
Reduced	10
Ended altogether	11
Don't know	12
	100%

QUESTION: Now, I'm going to read you several things you sometimes hear people say, and ask whether, in general, you agree or disagree. . . .

The Federal Government has a responsibility to try to reduce unemployment.

Agree	75%
Disagree	18
Don't know	7
	100%

The Federal Government has a responsibility to try to do away with poverty in this country.

Agree	72%
Disagree	20
Don't know	8
	100%

Although the question about Federal aid to education clearly raised the bogey of Federal dictation in the educational field by including payment of teachers' salaries, more than six out of ten were in favor of Federal assistance even in this sensitive area. When Congress passed the Medicare bill subsequent to our 1964 survey, a large majority of the American people were clearly behind it. There was obviously strong public backing for public housing and for Federal aid to rebuild cities and eliminate slums. Although our survey was conducted before many specific anti-poverty programs had been advanced, it showed that strong public support could be mobilized for "the war on poverty."

The Operational Spectrum

In order to group the attitudes of Americans toward Governmental programs at the operational level, a simple "Operational Spectrum" was devised. A respondent was classified as "completely liberal" if he gave favorable answers to all of the propositions mentioned above. He was rated as "completely conservative" if all of his answers were against the propositions. In between these two extremes, the Operational Spectrum provided categories for "predominantly liberal" (meaning the respondent was for most but not all of the propositions listed); "middle of the road" (meaning he was in favor of about half and disfavored the other half); and "predominantly conservative" (meaning he was against most but not all).* The distribution of the total sample based on this classification was:

* A more complete, technical description of the Operational Spectrum is given in Appendix C, pp. 207 f.

Operational Spectru

Completely liberal
Predominantly liberal
Middle of the road
Predominantly conservative
Completely conservative

In brief, about two-thirds of the public
with respect to the operational level
grams and the category of "complete
bered the "predominantly liberal" by m
  The figures fluctuated significantly a
ments of the population.* For example,
predominance in all occupational groups
side, there was among professional and
smaller proportion of liberals, either
dominant (54 per cent), than among the
centage among farmers (58 per cent) was
By comparison, three-fourths of the b
qualified as liberals. In large metropo
people were decidedly liberal; they were
in medium-size cities; people in towns an
the least liberal. In terms of regions, while
people living in the East were liberals, su
the next highest proportion of liberals (6
the Southern states that gave Johnson a ma
election. That figure was even higher tha
(62 per cent) or the West (59 per cent). Tl
age of liberals and the highest of conserv

* See Table 1 in Appendix F, pp. 215 ff. Party di
other domestic matters, as well as those based on
origin, will be discussed in Chapter IX on "Polit
pp. 134 ff.

Agree	72%
Disagree	20
Don't know	8
	100%

Although the question about Federal aid to education clearly raised the bogey of Federal dictation in the educational field by including payment of teachers' salaries, more than six out of ten were in favor of Federal assistance even in this sensitive area. When Congress passed the Medicare bill subsequent to our 1964 survey, a large majority of the American people were clearly behind it. There was obviously strong public backing for public housing and for Federal aid to rebuild cities and eliminate slums. Although our survey was conducted before many specific anti-poverty programs had been advanced, it showed that strong public support could be mobilized for "the war on poverty."

The Operational Spectrum

In order to group the attitudes of Americans toward Governmental programs at the operational level, a simple "Operational Spectrum" was devised. A respondent was classified as "completely liberal" if he gave favorable answers to all of the propositions mentioned above. He was rated as "completely conservative" if all of his answers were against the propositions. In between these two extremes, the Operational Spectrum provided categories for "predominantly liberal" (meaning the respondent was for most but not all of the propositions listed); "middle of the road" (meaning he was in favor of about half and disfavored the other half); and "predominantly conservative" (meaning he was against most but not all).* The distribution of the total sample based on this classification was:

* A more complete, technical description of the Operational Spectrum is given in Appendix C, pp. 207 f.

Operational Spectrum

Completely liberal	44%	⎱ 65%
Predominantly liberal	21	⎰
Middle of the road	21	} 21
Predominantly conservative	7	⎱ 14
Completely conservative	7	⎰
	100%	

In brief, about two-thirds of the public qualified as "liberal" with respect to the operational level of Government programs and the category of "completely liberal" outnumbered the "predominantly liberal" by more than two to one.

The figures fluctuated significantly among different elements of the population.* For example, although the heavy predominance in all occupational groups was on the liberal side, there was among professional and business people a smaller proportion of liberals, either complete or predominant (54 per cent), than among the rest; and the percentage among farmers (58 per cent) was only slightly higher. By comparison, three-fourths of the blue-collar workers qualified as liberals. In large metropolitan centers the people were decidedly liberal; they were only slightly less so in medium-size cities; people in towns and rural areas were the least liberal. In terms of regions, while 72 per cent of the people living in the East were liberals, surprisingly enough the next highest proportion of liberals (67 per cent) was in the Southern states that gave Johnson a majority in the 1964 election. That figure was even higher than in the Midwest (62 per cent) or the West (59 per cent). The lowest percentage of liberals and the highest of conservatives were to be

---

* See Table 1 in Appendix F, pp. 215 ff. Party differences on this and other domestic matters, as well as those based on religion and ethnic origin, will be discussed in Chapter IX on "Political Identifications," pp. 134 ff.

found in those Southern states that went for Goldwater in 1964.*

Fewer people fifty years of age or over were liberal than were those below fifty. The results were markedly stratified on the basis of education: the greatest proportion of liberals (three-fourths) were among respondents with only a grade school education; the least (one-half) were among the college-educated. There were related differences based on income: the proportion of liberals being very high among poorer people (three-fourths) and lowest among those with an annual income of $10,000 or over (one-half). The Negroes, who in 1964 were of course both relatively poor and uneducated, were phenomenally liberal (nine out of ten), with eight out of ten qualifying as "completely liberal."

Class Identifications

As sharp as the differences were in terms of education and income, they were even more marked on the basis of class identification—that is, according to the socioeconomic class with which respondents associated themselves. As earlier studies have shown,[4] this psychological identification is a state of mind which does not necessarily agree with objective criteria such as education, income, and occupation, customarily used for judging socioeconomic status. For example, in our survey more than one-fourth of those with incomes of $10,000 a year or more identified their interests with the "working class," as they defined this term, while more than one-fifth of those with incomes under $3,000 as-

* In this study, we divided the South into the five states that gave Goldwater a majority in 1964, on the one hand, and the eight that went for Johnson, on the other. For the listings, see the notes at the beginning of Appendix F, p. 214.

sociated themselves with the "middle class." Similarly, three out of ten of the professional and business group identified with the "working class," while more than one-third of the blue-collar workers saw themselves as members of the "middle class." The question used and the overall results it yielded were as follows:

> QUESTION: In the field of politics and government do you feel that your own interests are similar to the interests of the propertied class, the middle class, or the working class?

Propertied class	5%
Middle class	37
Working class	53
Don't know	5
	100%

Since the basic outlook of most individuals toward governmental affairs is conditioned, to some extent, by what each conceives to be the interests of the class to which he feels he belongs, it comes as no surprise that there were marked variations on the Operational Spectrum by class identification. The percentages of operational liberals in the three groups were as follows:

Identify with	*Per cent liberals*
Propertied class	40%
Middle class	57
Working class	74

The Use of Governmental Power

The configuration of attitudes concerning Governmental programs, as tested by our Operational Spectrum, is borne out by the results on a more abstract, general question about Government power.

QUESTION: Which one of the statements listed on this card comes closest to your own views about Government power today?

1. The Federal Government today has too much power.   26%

2. The Federal Government is now using just about the right amount of power for meeting today's needs.   36

3. The Federal Government should use its powers even more vigorously to promote the well-being of all segments of the people.   31

Don't know.   7

     —— 100%

These somewhat surprising results indicate that the cliché about the Government's having too much power—which many people assume is deeply ingrained in American thinking—is not valid. For, as shown in the table, only one-fourth of the public accepted the view that the Federal Government's power is excessive, while two-thirds believed it is about right or that the Government should use its power even more vigorously. Perhaps the underlying feeling about this matter was summed up by a Republican housewife in California who said, "I don't think it (the Government) has any more power than we have given it or allowed it to take." It will be noted that the 67 per cent endorsing the present amount of Government power, or even more, corresponds very closely with the 65 per cent who were either completely or predominantly liberal on the Operational Spectrum. Again, if the realistic test of liberalism *vs.* conservatism under today's conditions is relative willingness or reluctance to see Governmental power and resources utilized to accomplish social objectives, these results confirm the liberal consensus among Americans.

Certainly, no one would expect a perfect correlation between categories on the Operational Spectrum and the more abstract question about Governmental power, but the correspondence is quite close. The relationship is shown in Table II-1, with the "don't knows" excluded.

TABLE II-1

OPERATIONAL SPECTRUM BY GOVERNMENTAL POWER

	Government has too much power	Government power about right	Government should use more power
Operational Spectrum			
Completely liberal	7%	44%	49%
Predominantly liberal	19	46	35
Middle of the road	45	36	19
Predominantly conservative	69	25	6
Completely conservative	89	11	*

* Less than one-half of one per cent

If the center and right-hand columns in the table are combined, it turns out that nine out of ten of those who were completely liberal on the Operational Spectrum favored the Federal Government's using at least the amount of power it had then, while the same proportion of those who were completely conservative believed the Government already had too much power. Between these two extremes the figures follow logical directional patterns.

As would be anticipated, demographic differences on this general question about Governmental power followed roughly the same patterns as they did on the Operational Spectrum.* The conservative answer that the Federal Gov-

* See Table 2 in Appendix F, pp. 218 ff.

ernment has too much power received least support among
Negroes, only one-fiftieth of whom concurred, and less than
average support among blue-collar workers and the 21–29
age group (one-fifth in both cases). Support was strong
among the well-to-do (one-third) and particularly among the
closely related college-educated (two-fifths). The sentiment
that the Government has too much power was low in the
metropolitan centers and increased markedly as the size of
urban units decreased, reaching a peak in the small towns
and rural areas. By regions, it was weakest in the East (one-
fifth) and phenomenally strong in those Southern states that
went for Goldwater in 1964 (more than one-half).

The extremely liberal sentiment that the Government
should use its powers even more vigorously also deserves
comment. It was much more prevalent than average among
those with only a grade school education and people with
incomes of less than $5,000 per year, and spectacularly so
among Negro Americans. These groups obviously felt more
need for Governmental help and were least afraid of Governmental power; finding their situation too difficult to
cope with by themselves, they considered the Government
their best hope. The belief that the Government should ex-
ercise its powers even more vigorously was also more prevalent than average among young people, among those who
identified their interests with the "working class," among
people living in large and medium-size cities, and in the
East—all of these being groups where more liberals were
found on the Operational Spectrum.

The Welfare State

From the results reported in this chapter, the conclusion
clearly emerges that about two-thirds of the American
people have assumptions which lead them to perceive the
utilization of the power and resources of the Federal Gov-

ernment as a good and proper way to achieve a wide range of social purposes. And the more an individual's own purposes are furthered by such Government action, the greater is his feeling that such action is legitimate and desirable. As a housewife in Norfolk put it when asked about her worries and fears: "I don't worry about nothing. It doesn't get you anywhere. I think there are people to take care of the future. The President and his workers are going to do what they can to help us." Negro Americans, with their low incomes, lower education, and with relatively few members in the nation's business and professional life, feel the need for help most keenly and are strongest in their approval of Governmental action for social ends.

In brief, as of 1964 a large majority of Americans were congenial to the practical operations required to attain and improve the welfare state. In this sense, at the operational level of Government programs, President Johnson was correct when he indicated that the argument over the welfare state had been resolved in favor of Federal action to achieve it.

III

Ideological Outlooks

The Role and Sphere of Government

The good Lord raised up this mighty Republic to be a home for the brave and to flourish as the land of the free— not to stagnate in the swampland of collectivism. . . . The whole history of freedom has been simply the history of resistance to the concentration of power in government. (Barry Goldwater in *Where I Stand*.)

We are now 90 per cent socialistic. We're losing more freedoms all the time. We have far too much big government. (The wife of a Federal employee in Michigan.)

Who was it said that it's a good thing we don't get all the government we pay for? (A public utility executive in California.)

The people are being taxed too much. The government wastes too much. Also, the Federal Government has its hand in everything. (A Nebraska fireman.)

Return to the grass roots of our ancestors' beliefs. (A Florida contractor.)

We need a form of government like we once had in the days of President Hoover. (An engineer living in Texas.)

More like it was in the past—in McKinley's day. (A seventy-nine-year-old widow in Baltimore.)

The liberal consensus of Americans at the *operational* level revealed in the last chapter fades away when the views of the same representative sample of people are tapped at the *ideological* level.

This is clearly shown by the following results obtained from questions concerned with some of the abstract ideas that make up the American political ideology having to do with the proper role and sphere of government in general and of the Federal Government in particular.

QUESTION: Now, I'm going to read several statements you sometimes hear, and ask whether, in general, you agree or disagree. . . .

The Federal Government is interfering too much in state and local matters.

Agree	40%
Disagree	47
Don't know	13
	100%

Social problems here in this country could be solved more effectively if the government would only keep its hands off and let people in local communities handle their own problems in their own ways.

Agree	49%
Disagree	38
Don't know	13
	100%

The government has gone too far in regulating business and interfering with the free enterprise system.

Agree	42%
Disagree	39
Don't know	19
	100%

The government is interfering too much with property rights.

Agree	39%
Disagree	37
Don't know	24
	100%

There is a definite trend toward socialism in this country.

Agree	46%
Disagree	22
Don't know	32
	100%

There is too much Communist and left-wing influence in our Government these days.

Agree	47%
Disagree	30
Don't know	23
	100%

From the answers to these questions concerned with abstract ideas about government, it will be seen that not only is there no consensus on the liberal side, but in fact, in most cases the predominance tends to be at least slightly on the conservative side.

Ideology and Social Welfare

The abstract concepts Americans tend to hold about the nature and functioning of our socioeconomic system are even more pronouncedly conservative than their notions about the role and sphere of government. For example, here is the way the people interviewed reacted to one of the statements put to them:

> STATEMENT: Generally speaking, any able-bodied person who really wants to work in this country can find a job and earn a living.

Agree	76%
Disagree	21
Don't know	3
	100%

The hard fact is that at the time these interviews were conducted the unemployment rate was in excess of 5 per cent of the labor force, and among Negro Americans considerably higher than 15 per cent. Most of these people were able-bodied and most of them wanted to work. Nevertheless they could not find jobs because of economic conditions in general and lack of education, training, and skills in particular. In view of the statistical evidence to the contrary, the notion that, generally speaking, any able-bodied person who really wants to work can find a job is little short of a myth.

Yet even among the lower income group (with family incomes of less than $5,000 a year), whose members are closest to the realities of the unemployment situation, seven out of ten agreed with the statement that, generally speaking, any able-bodied person who really wants to work can find a job. When the statistical evidence on unemployment among Negroes is kept in mind, the fact that six out of ten of them also agreed, with only one in three disagreeing, is a further demonstration of the extraordinary credence accorded this particular aspect of American mythology.

With this assumption about the availability of job opportunities, it is little wonder that great skepticism was found about the unemployed and their qualifications for government relief.

> STATEMENT: The relief rolls are loaded with chiselers and people who just don't want to work.*

Agree	66%
Disagree	23
Don't know	11
	100%

The feelings expressed about this matter were often vehement:

> Now people won't work for fear of losing government handouts. (A retired grocer in Texas.)

> We need to do something about this welfare business. If people don't want to work, they shouldn't be fed. (A Government employee in Arizona.)

> Establish CCC camps again. And, instead of these people standing around drawing relief, make them work for it. There's plenty of jobs for them that need doing. Let's quit handing everything out on a platter. (A millwright in Michigan.)

Even among those with family incomes of less than $5,000 a year, six out of ten agreed that the relief rolls are loaded with chiselers and people who just don't want to work. And among Negroes, who as a group unquestionably have had more experience with relief than any other element of

* According to White House aide Joseph A. Califano, Jr. (*New York Times:* April 20, 1967), a Government study has shown that only about 50,000 of the 7.3 million persons on public welfare are "employable," that is to say capable of being given job skills and training that will make them self-sufficient. The rest are either mothers or children, or are blind, aged, or handicapped.

the population, the "agree" percentage (43 per cent) slightly exceeded the "disagree" figure (39 per cent).

This pervading cynicism about those on relief tended to carry over to the poor in general. A large majority thought that lack of effort, either alone or combined with circumstances, is at the root of poverty, rather than circumstances alone.

QUESTION: In your opinion, which is generally more often to blame if a person is poor—lack of effort on his part, or circumstances beyond his control?

Circumstances	25%
Lack of effort	34
Both	38
Don't know	3
	100%

Almost three-fourths of the total population felt that the poor are at least partially to blame for their own situation, a reflection no doubt of the deeply embedded Puritan belief that whereas virtue is rewarded in material ways, poverty is evidence of sin. (As Henry Ward Beecher once put it: "No man in this land suffers from poverty unless it be more than his fault—unless it be his sin.") This belief was alluded to in an unusually thoughtful comment on the problem by a public relations woman living in a suburb of Washington, D.C.:

I think we're still awfully sort of Calvinistic and moralistic in our approach toward caring for our people. The kind of thing that Goldwater is talking about now reflects an attitude on the part of Americans that everybody has got a moral, not a right, but a duty to supply himself and his family with everything they need without help from anybody else. And, if he's unable to do that, he's somehow some kind of a crook. And I think this attitude in this country has got to change because, the world being the way it is, everybody *can't* be responsible for himself. All too often, they are at the mercy of forces they have no control over and can't understand.

Sure, in a way, it's the fault of the poor that they are poor because they have no ability to do any better. Lots of them don't have enough education to hold better jobs. Lots of them never had a family which gave them any incentive to work hard or get a better job. Lots of them have poor health. Lots of them are culturally deprived so they wouldn't even know how to take advantage of education if it were given them. They can't even—you know, the illiterates—read and follow simple instructions. It's very hard for them to hold down anything above the most menial jobs. And then a lot of them just don't have any hope because they've come of a long line of people who never had any hope and they don't *expect* anything better. And when you don't have hope, you don't really try very hard. So maybe it's their fault, then, but you've got to take people's background into consideration when you say whether it's their fault or not.

As Table III-1 shows, while a plurality of the well-to-do ascribed poverty simply to lack of effort, a majority of the

TABLE III-1

CAUSES OF POVERTY BY FAMILY INCOME

	Under $5,000	$5,000-$9,999	$10,000 and over
Circumstances	28%	23%	23%
Lack of effort	25	38	44
Both	43	36	32
Don't know	4	3	1
	100%	100%	100%

poor also agreed that they were at least partially to blame for their own condition either because of lack of effort or lack of effort plus circumstances.

The reactions of a huge majority to another of the statements included in our questionnaire are related to this dominant belief in the culpability of the poor:

STATEMENT: We should rely more on individual initiative and not so much on governmental welfare programs.

Agree	79%
Disagree	12
Don't know	9
	100%

Although the members of the lower income group were not as enthusiastic about this proposition as the well-to-do, still seven out of ten of them agreed, as did six out of ten Negro Americans, for whom governmental welfare programs are no doubt more important than they are to any other element of the population.

In short, in view of actual practices at the operational level, Americans at the ideological level continue to pay lip service to an amazing degree to stereotypes and shibboleths inherited from the past. The abstract ideas they tend to hold about the nature and functioning of our socioeconomic system still seem to stem more from the underlying assumptions of a laissez-faire philosophy than from the operating assumptions of the New Deal, the Fair Deal, the New Frontier, or the Great Society.

The apprehensions of many Americans about the New-Deal-to-Great-Society trend were exemplified by the following comments:

I fear the tendency toward a welfare state with so many thinking the government owes them a living. (The wife of an airline employee living in Illinois.)

If individualism is completely destroyed, I'm afraid that there could be too much leaning on the Federal Government and individual rights and individual responsibility will end altogether. (A housewife in the State of Washington.)

I feel the people have lost their sense of initiative and responsibility. They prefer to let the government do their thinking for them. (A private detective in Florida.)

If the U.S. continues on its present course, the inevitable will mean total domination by the state. . . . It will be a Godless state with the only drive being a dictatorshiplike power. (A Navy man living in Virginia.)

The Ideological Spectrum

An Ideological Spectrum was set up along lines similar to the Operational Spectrum to make general groupings possible. This procedure rated respondents according to their reactions to five statements previously listed, some having to do with ideological conceptions of the proper role and sphere of government and some with abstract ideas about the nature and functioning of our socioeconomic system. These provided a rough index of the degree to which respondents accepted or rejected the traditional American conservative ideology. The five statements were as follows:

1. The Federal Government is interfering too much in state and local matters.
2. The government has gone too far in regulating business and interfering with the free enterprise system.
3. Social problems here in this country could be solved more effectively if the government would only keep its hands off and let people in local communities handle their own problems in their own ways.
4. Generally speaking, any able-bodied person who really wants to work in this country can find a job and earn a living.

5. We should rely more on individual initiative and ability and not so much on governmental welfare programs.

Under our scheme, a person who agreed with all of these propositions was rated "completely conservative" and one who disagreed as "completely liberal." In between these extremes, the Ideological Spectrum provided categories for "predominantly conservative" (meaning the respondent agreed with most but not all); "middle of the road" (meaning he agreed with about half and disagreed with about half); and "predominantly liberal" (meaning he disagreed with most but not all).* The results are given in Table III-2. The figures obtained on the Operational Spectrum are repeated for comparative purposes.

TABLE III-2
IDEOLOGICAL AND OPERATIONAL SPECTRUMS

	Ideological Spectrum		Operational Spectrum	
Completely liberal	4%	} 16%	44%	} 65%
Predominantly liberal	12		21	
Middle of the road	34	} 34	21	} 21
Predominantly conservative	20	} 50	7	} 14
Completely conservative	30		7	
	100%		100%	

This table is of the utmost importance for an understanding of conflicting aspects of the political orientations of Americans. It will be seen that while 65 per cent of our sample were liberal on the Operational Spectrum, only 16 per cent were either completely or predominantly liberal on the Ideological Spectrum. Conversely, while only 14 per cent

* A more complete, technical description of the Ideological Spectrum is given in Appendix D, pp. 209 f.

were conservative on the Operational Spectrum, one-half were in one or the other of the conservative categories on the Ideological Spectrum. This discrepancy between operational outlooks and ideological views is so marked as to be almost schizoid.

Demographic Patterns

Since the overall results on the Ideological Spectrum are what they are, it follows, of course, that the figures for each population subgroup are skewed much more toward the dominant conservative side than was the case with the Operational Spectrum. Within this context, the demographic patterns that emerge on the Ideological Spectrum are similar in some respects to those on the Operational Spectrum and different in others.*

The top income group and the college-educated were somewhat more conservative on the Ideological Spectrum than the lower groups, just as they were much less liberal on the Operational Spectrum. However, at the ideological level, the differences between the upper and lower groups were slight in the percentage of conservatives. This would seem at first to confirm the common impression that, whereas in some European countries ideological differences between socioeconomic classes are acute, in the United States class differences in ideology are relatively slight. But it turns out that, while this appears to be the case if economic status is measured by such objective indices as education and income, it is not so when the factor of subjective class identification is introduced.

It will be remembered that the question discussed in the preceding chapter asked whether, in the field of politics and government, those interviewed identified their own interests

---

* The figures are given in Table 3 in Appendix F, pp. 220 ff.

with the propertied class, the middle class, or the working class. As Table III-3 shows, marked differences at the ideological level emerged on the basis of these differing class identifications. The proportion of conservatives among those associating their own interests with the propertied class was half again as great as among those who identified with the working class; and the difference in the number of conservatives between those who identified with the middle class and with the working class was considerable. At the same time, it must be pointed out that even among the latter group the percentage of ideological conservatives was more than double the percentage of ideological liberals.

Age differences were even more pronounced on the Ideological than on the Operational Spectrum. The proportion of ideological conservatives among those fifty and over (59 per cent) was very much greater than among the middle and younger age groups (45 per cent and 43 per cent respectively). It is no doubt to be expected that older people, most of whom went through their formative years prior to the New Deal, would tend to give even greater credence to the traditional American ideology. The differences on an occupational basis were also marked, with approximately 60 per cent of the farmers and "non-labor" * respondents qualifying as ideological conservatives compared with only 45 per cent of the blue-collar workers. Somewhat surprisingly, however, among the professional and business people, who were the least liberal of all the occupational groups on the Opera-

---

* As explained at the beginning of Appendix F, p. 213, the "non-labor" category consists primarily of households headed by retired people and, to a lesser extent, by housewives, students, or the physically handicapped. One of its chief peculiarities is that, in our sample, 85 percent of those in this category were fifty years of age or over, as compared with a national average of 40 percent of the adult population.

TABLE III-3

IDEOLOGICAL SPECTRUM BY CLASS IDENTIFICATION

	Identify Interests with		
	Propertied Class	Middle Class	Working Class
Ideological Spectrum			
Completely or predominantly liberal	4%	13%	21%
Middle of the road	33	32	35
Completely or predominantly conservative	63	55	44
	100%	100%	100%

tional Spectrum, the percentage of ideological conservatives was almost as low as among the workers.

Regional variations were also enormous. The percentage of conservatives dropped from more than eight out of ten in the Southern states that voted for Goldwater in 1964 to only four out of ten in the East. On the basis of city size, just as the proportion of liberals on the Operational Spectrum dropped, so the percentage of conservatives on the Ideological Spectrum rose as one moved from the huge metropolitan areas to the larger cities, to the towns, and, finally, to the countryside.

The greatest difference of all on the Ideological Spectrum seemed to derive from racial and religious background. Along with the Jews, Negro Americans were the only group whose percentage of ideological liberals was actually greater by a wide margin than the percentage of conservatives. Primarily this was because large majorities of Negroes—unlike the whites—disagreed with the following three propositions included in the rating system for the Ideological Spectrum:

The Federal Government is interfering too much in state and local matters.

The government has gone too far in regulating business and interfering with the free enterprise system.

Social problems here in this country could be solved more effectively if the government would only keep its hands off and let people in local communities handle their own problems in their own ways.

The Negroes' disagreement with these three statements, taken in conjunction with the huge majority who qualified as liberal on the Operational Spectrum and who felt the Federal Government should use its powers even more vigorously, reinforces the conclusion that American Negroes tend to see government action, particularly action by the Federal Government, as the most effective way—indeed, perhaps the only way—to remedy the problems besetting them.

Operational Liberals, Ideological Conservatives

The explanation for the discrepancy between results on the Operational Spectrum, which revealed a consensus on the liberal side, and those on the Ideological Spectrum, which leaned toward the conservative side, lies in the fact that 23 percent of Americans are both ideological conservatives and at the same time operational liberals. Table III-4, in which the two liberal and the two conservative categories have been combined, shows a high degree of consistency in this respect on the part of the ideological liberals: nine out of ten of them qualify as liberals on the Operational Spectrum. However, among the ideological conservatives, almost one-half proved to be operational liberals. Commager described these ideological conservatives who are operational liberals to a tee in this comment about Americans in general: "They clung to the vocabulary of laissez-faire, yet

TABLE III-4

OPERATIONAL SPECTRUM BY IDEOLOGICAL SPECTRUM

	Ideological Spectrum		
	Liberal	Middle of Road	Conservative
Operational Spectrum			
Liberal	90%	78%	46%
Middle of the road	9	18	28
Conservative	1	4	26
	100%	100%	100%

faithfully supplied the money and the personnel for vastly expanded governmental activities." [5]

As compared with a national figure of 23 per cent, the proportion of those exhibiting this schizoid combination of operational liberalism with ideological conservatism was very much higher than average among those with only a grade school education (30 per cent) and the very poor (28 per cent), as well as among people living in the South, and particularly in the Southern states that went for Goldwater in 1964 (41 per cent). Conversely, the least schizoid groups were the college-educated (14 per cent), the well-to-do (17 per cent), the professional and business people (13 per cent), people living in large cities (18 per cent), and, above all, Jews (12 per cent) and Negroes (12 per cent), who showed throughout our study greater consistency in their views than any other groups.

A similar picture emerges in answers to the question whether the Federal Government has too much power, about the right amount, or should use its powers even more vigorously. Logic would require that anyone who qualified as liberal on the Ideological Spectrum (because he disagreed with all or most of the conservative-oriented propositions that made up that score) should also have felt that the Government has about the right amount of power or should use its powers even more vigorously. Table III-5 shows great consistency in this respect: almost all of the ideological liberals adopted one or the other of these positions regarding Governmental power.

However, the only logical answer that could be given to this question by a respondent rated conservative on the Ideological Spectrum was that the Government has too much power. Yet, as will be seen in Table III-5, only half of the

TABLE III-5
GOVERNMENT POWER BY IDEOLOGICAL SPECTRUM

	Liberal	Middle of Road	Conservative
Governmental Power			
Government has too much power	3%	6%	52%
Government has right amount of power	43 ⎫	53 ⎫	32 ⎫
Government should use more power	54 ⎬ 97%	41 ⎬ 94%	16 ⎬ 48%
	100%	100%	100%

ideological conservatives gave this answer; almost as many said either that the Government has about the right amount of power or should use its powers even more actively. This confirms the conclusion that a great many ideological conservatives are, in practice, willing to see Government power and resources used to accomplish social objectives.

Lack of Ideological Foundations

In conclusion, we return to the broad perspective. The political orientations of half the American people are conservative as judged from the Ideological Spectrum, a fact that reflects their abstract and conceptual assumptions concerning the proper sphere and role of government and the nature and functioning of the American socioeconomic system. At the same time, in the case of a large proportion of those who hold them, these conservative ideological assumptions conflict with their liberal operational assumptions, so that their overall political orientations appear to be an inconsistent mixture. This ambivalence, characterizing the thought of many Americans, is illustrated by the remarks of a salesman living in Oregon. When asked about his wishes and hopes for the future, he expressed the desire that "something be done for the poor, for the elderly and for people on relief." Yet when, a few moments later, he was queried about his worries and fears for the country, he replied: "That the government will keep on spending over their income. If this doesn't end, we'll be taxed to death." Similarly, a mechanic living in Texas first said, "We are drifting toward a socialist form of government—and that could be good. It might mean more and better jobs." But a moment afterward he was complaining that the Government already had too much power.

Complete *ideological* conformity with the trend of policies and programs represented by the New Deal, the Fair Deal, the New Frontier, and the Great Society is limited to the small minority of 16 per cent who qualified as liberals on the Ideological Spectrum. The generally conservative stance at the ideological level indicates that the liberal trend of policies and programs that has characterized the American scene much of the time since the early days of Franklin Roosevelt's New Deal has little secure underlying foundation in any ideological consensus. For example, so long as three-fourths of the public believe that, generally speaking, any able-bodied person can find a job and earn a living, it can hardly be argued that there is solid popular support for large elements of the "war on poverty" programs or similar programs yet to come. As a Massachusetts business executive saw the problem: "I am afraid that we are too frightened of the word socialism, and that there will be a reaction to programs to help people because people misunderstand this as socialism."

While the old argument about the "welfare state" has long since been resolved at the operational level of Government programs, it most definitely *has not* been resolved at the ideological level. A good many Americans still see the past with nostalgia, as did this investment counselor in California:

> I would like things to be more simple, not so complex— not to be burdened down with bills, like freeways, not for the U.S. to be involved in so many things. They shouldn't be so concerned about Vietnam and poverty. It makes for more complex government. I'd like to see a simple government, not having so much to think about.

IV

Self-Identification As
Liberal or Conservative

Self-Styled "Liberals" and "Conservatives"

In addition to classifying the sample population on the Operational and Ideological Spectrums, we also obtained the people's own testimony as to where they thought they belonged on the liberal-conservative scale.

QUESTION: Which one of the phrases on this card do you think best describes you yourself when it comes to political matters?

Very liberal	6%	} 26%
Moderately liberal	20	
Middle of the road	34	} 34
Moderately conservative	24	} 30
Very conservative	6	
Don't know	10	
	100%	

It is noteworthy that few Americans classify themselves as either very liberal or very conservative; the tendency is towards the center. It is also significant that the middle-of-the-road position did not prove more popular than it did.

41

It was almost equalled by the combined conservative categories. The liberal label was somewhat less popular.

In only three groups did a plurality of individuals pin the "liberal" label on themselves—Negro Americans, Jews, and people of Eastern or Central European descent. It will be remembered that the first two of these groups were the only ones which showed more liberals than conservatives on the Ideological Spectrum. In the case of all other elements of the population, either "middle of the road" or "conservative" designations were in the ascendancy.* As would be expected, the percentage of those identifying themselves as conservatives rose as education and income went up and, on an occupational basis, was highest among the professional and business group. However, the fact that there were fewer conservatives among those with lower income and less education as well as among the blue-collar workers did not mean that more of them considered themselves to be liberals. Instead, among those able to classify themselves, a higher proportion pinned the "middle of the road" rather than the "liberal" label on themselves. The picture with respect to blue-collar workers in general changed, however, in the case of the more limited group of union members. Among them the "liberal" figure was as high as the "middle of the road" (35 per cent in both cases) and a great deal higher than the "conservative" (23 per cent).

As would also be expected, the percentage of self-designated conservatives was significantly higher among those fifty years of age and over than among those 30–49, and particularly among those 21–29, where an unusually high "middle of the road" proportion emerged. By regions, the highest percentage of people labelling themselves conservative was in the Southern states where Goldwater won a ma-

* The figures are given in Table 4 in Appendix F, pp. 222 f.

jority in 1964, and the lowest was in the East. Conversely, the lowest proportion of liberals was in Goldwater's South, followed by the rest of the South; by far the highest proportion of liberals was in the East, but, even in the East, the "middle of the road" figure was somewhat higher than the "liberal" figure. Respondents in towns of under 50,000 population and in rural areas were markedly more conservative than those in metropolitan areas and cities, where there was a much higher percentage of those who called themselves liberal although still no plurality.

Classification of 1964 Presidential Candidates

In addition to identifying themselves as liberal, middle of the road, or conservative, the sample population was asked to place Lyndon Johnson and Barry Goldwater on the liberal-conservative spectrum. The results seem to show considerable confusion in the public mind about the meaning of these terms. For, realistically speaking, with respect to the operational level of government programs, Johnson could only be classified as "liberal" and Goldwater as "conservative." Furthermore, in the 1964 Presidential campaign when our interviewing was done, the ideological differences between the two candidates were as clear-cut as they ever get in modern American politics. Goldwater hewed to the conservative line with little, if any, temporizing. His positions, both before and during the campaign, were thoroughly consistent with the affirmative side of the five propositions on which our Ideological Spectrum was based. Johnson, on the other hand, was a New Deal protegé, the inheritor of President Kennedy's New Frontier policies, and, later, the originator of his own Great Society programs. His entire posture involved the negation of each and every one of the statements used for the Ideological Spectrum. Thus, either from the operational or the ideological point of view, logic required that Johnson be labelled a "liberal" or, at the very least, "middle of the road," but certainly not "conservative"; and that Goldwater be designated a "conservative," not "middle of the road" and definitely not "liberal."

People with a high degree of politically relevant information tended to agree strongly with this assessment of the two men. To probe such knowledge, our survey included a battery of questions, varying in degree of difficulty, to test what people knew about domestic and international matters. On the domestic side, people were asked to identify Chief Justice Earl Warren and Senator William J. Fulbright. Respondents were also required to name the men who were then running for Vice President on the Republican ticket (Miller) and on the Democratic ticket (Humphrey). On the more difficult side, they were then asked who ran with Nixon as the Vice Presidential candidate on the Republican ticket in 1960 (Lodge). And, finally, they were confronted with this tough query:

> QUESTION: If anything should happen to President Johnson before the elections in November, do you happen to know who would succeed him and serve out his present term as President?

The correct answer, of course, was the Speaker of the House of Representatives (McCormack). Those six items were used to rate people on a Domestic Information Score, with the following overall results:

Well informed (5 or 6 correct answers)	28%
Moderately informed (3 or 4 correct answers)	35
Uninformed (0 to 2 correct answers)	37
	100%

It should be noted that more than one-third of the United States population is perhaps too uninformed politically to participate intelligently in the democratic process.* But at this stage of our story, the point is that the well informed agreed with the assessment of the two candidates made above: 65 per cent categorized Johnson as "liberal" and 25 per cent as "middle of the road," while 77 per cent called Goldwater a "conservative" and 46 per cent said he was "very conservative."

But when the evaluations of the moderately informed and the uninformed were included, the picture becomes much more foggy. The results for the sample as a whole are given in Table IV-1. Only 50 per cent identified Goldwater as

TABLE IV-1

JOHNSON AND GOLDWATER ON LIBERAL-CONSERVATIVE SPECTRUM

	Johnson		Goldwater	
Very liberal	18%	} 47%	5%	} 11%
Moderately liberal	29		6	
Middle of the road	29	} 29	16	} 16
Moderately conservative	10	} 15	22	} 50
Very conservative	5		28	
Don't know	9		23	
	100%		100%	

either moderately or very conservative, and, incredibly enough, 11 per cent saw him as a liberal. On the other hand, only 47 per cent considered Johnson a liberal; and 15 per cent called him a conservative—a designation he could conceivably have earned only in his gesture of frugality in turning out the lights at the White House.

The fuzzy thinking revealed by such results inevitably raises the question as to what individuals had in mind when

* Less than half of U.S. voters can name the Congressman representing their own district (Gallup: August 26, 1966).

they labelled themselves and the candidates "liberal," "middle of the road," or "conservative." The great majority of people thought they understood and could apply these terms, as shown by the fact that, when asked to identify themselves, only 6 per cent replied "don't know" and only 9 per cent felt unable to classify Johnson to their own satisfaction.

Correlations with Ideological and Operational Spectrums

Some light may be thrown on the criteria respondents had in mind when they classified themselves and the two candidates on the liberal-conservative scale by referring again to the results on the Operational and Ideological Spectrums. For comparative purposes, Table IV-2 gives the overall fig-

TABLE IV-2

OPERATIONAL AND IDEOLOGICAL SPECTRUMS AND SELF-IDENTIFICATION
AS LIBERAL OR CONSERVATIVE

	Operational Spectrum	Self-Identification	Ideological Spectrum
Liberal	65%	29%	16%
Middle of the road	21	38	34
Conservative	14	33	50
	100%	100%	100%

ures on the last two spectrums, along with those on the self-identification question, excluding the "don't knows." While all these percentages have been given before, when they are put side by side it becomes readily apparent that results on the self-identification question fall midway between liberal dominance on the Operational Spectrum and conservative dominance on the Ideological Spectrum.

But, how does the way people classified themselves corre-
spond to their ratings on the two spectrums? Table IV-3

TABLE IV-3
IDEOLOGICAL SPECTRUM BY SELF-IDENTIFICATION AS LIBERAL OR
CONSERVATIVE

	Identified Self As		
	Liberal	Middle of Road	Conservative
Qualified on Ideological Spectrum As			
Liberal	28%	16%	7%
Middle Road	46	38	23
Conservative	26	46	70
	100%	100%	100%

shows the correspondence on the Ideological Spectrum. As
shown here, only 28 per cent of those who called themselves
"liberal" qualified as such on the Ideological Spectrum, and
almost an equal number of self-styled liberals actually qualified as ideological conservatives. Clearly, then, when people
think of themselves as "liberal," they are not thinking in
ideological terms: more than seven out of ten qualified either
as middle of the road or as conservative on the Ideological
Spectrum. On the other hand, people who call themselves
"conservative" do seem to have ideological concepts in mind,
for seven out of ten turn out as conservative on the Ideological Spectrum.

The other side of the coin is shown in Table IV-4, which
relates self-identification with the Operational Spectrum.
Here the startling fact emerges that more than four out of
ten self-designated "conservatives" actually qualified as liberal on the Operational Spectrum and only three in ten
stayed in the conservative column. It thus seems apparent

TABLE IV-4

OPERATIONAL SPECTRUM BY SELF-IDENTIFICATION AS LIBERAL OR CONSERVATIVE

	Identified Self As		
	Liberal	Middle of Road	Conservative
Qualified on *Operational Spectrum As*			
Liberal	81%	68%	44%
Middle Road	15	22	27
Conservative	4	10	29
	100%	100%	100%

that most people who think of themselves as conservative are not thinking of operational aspects of Government programs but are, as already noted, thinking of ideological considerations. On the other hand, the fact that eight out of ten of those who call themselves liberal actually do qualify as liberal on the Operational Spectrum, even though, as just shown, most of them rate as conservative or middle of the road on the Ideological Spectrum, indicates that it is precisely the area of Government programs of action that people are thinking about when they refer to themselves as "liberal."

A similar picture is evident in Table IV-5, where the liberal or conservative classification people gave themselves is compared with results on the question whether the Federal Government has too much power, about the right amount, or should use its power even more vigorously. Few of those calling themselves "liberal" thought the Government had too much power. However, among the conservatives, the same schizoid situation found before appears again: slightly more than half of the self-styled conservatives felt

TABLE IV-5

GOVERNMENT POWER BY SELF-IDENTIFICATION AS LIBERAL OR
CONSERVATIVE

| | Identified Self As | | |
	Liberal	Middle of Road	Conservative
Government has too much power	11%	24%	48%
Government has right amount of power	44 ⎱ 89%	44 ⎱ 76%	29 ⎱ 52%
Government should use more power	45 ⎰	32 ⎰	23 ⎰
	100%	100%	100%

the Government had about the right amount or should use
more power, instead of already having too much power.
While there was a consistency between the way liberals
classified themselves and their views about Government
power, half of the conservatives did not include this factor
in their definition of a conservative.

In brief, there appears to be little meeting of the minds
concerning a proper definition of "liberal" and "conservative" among those who designate themselves as one or the
other: the orientation of self-styled conservatives is chiefly
ideological, the orientation of self-styled liberals is chiefly
operational and pragmatic. From this and the preceding
chapter, the conclusion emerges that if one calls himself a
"liberal" or qualifies as such on the Ideological Spectrum,
the probability is high that he will also rate as a liberal on
the Operational Spectrum and will favor the use of Governmental power and resources to accomplish social objectives.
If he classifies himself as "middle of the road" or qualifies
as such on the Ideological Spectrum, the probabilities are
heavily in the same direction, although not quite as mark-

edly as among liberals. However, in the case of one who calls himself a "conservative" or who qualifies as a conservative on the Ideological Spectrum, there is a good chance that there will be an inconsistency between his ideological and his operational orientations: he is more likely than not to qualify as a liberal on the Operational Spectrum, and the probability is about fifty-fifty that he will feel the Government either has about the right amount of power or should use its powers even more vigorously.

In view of this demonstrated confusion, especially among conservatives, questions sometimes asked on surveys as to whether the Government or the President should be "conservative" or "liberal" or should go more to the "right" or to the "left" appear to be relatively meaningless. Little reference will be made in the remainder of this book to how people identified themselves on the liberal-conservative scale. We shall concentrate, instead, primarily upon the Operational Spectrum, which is the most significant from any functional point of view, and secondarily on the Ideological Spectrum.

V

The Concerns of Americans

For a large proportion of the American people, there is clearly not only a separation in but a conflict between their attitudes toward practical Governmental operations and programs, on the one hand, and their ideological ideas and abstract concepts about government and society, on the other. This conflict is resolved in a typically pragmatic American fashion: the practical is given precedence over the theoretical. At the operational level of government, the great majority of Americans are more concerned about practical problems than they are about abstract conceptions on the ideological level. They want government to work.[6]

This situation was revealed when people were asked how worried or concerned they were about a list of twenty-three issues or problems—a great deal, considerably, not very much, or not at all. To simplify tabulations, a weighting system was used: an answer of "not at all" was scored as zero; "not very much" as 100; "considerably" as 200; and "a great deal" as 300. Thus, in Table V-1, where the results are listed in rank order, the maximum possible degree of concern would be indicated by a score of 300; the minimum by a score of zero. The impression derived from an inspection of this table is that the American people are most con-

TABLE V-1

DEGREES OF CONCERN

	Average Scores
1. Keeping the country out of war	269
2. Combatting world Communism	257
3. Keeping our military defense strong	250
4. Controlling the use of nuclear weapons	248
5. Maintaining respect for the United States in other countries	244
6. Maintaining law and order a	240
7. Raising moral standards in this country	236
8. Improving our educational system	226
9. Relations with Russia	225
10. The problem of Communist China	223
11. Unemployment in the United States	218
12. Reducing poverty in this country	215
13. The problem of Vietnam b	214
14. Preserving our free enterprise system	213
15. Medicare for the elderly	207
16. Keeping NATO and our other alliances strong	205
17. Preserving our individual liberties against government interference	204
18. Government spending	203
19. Negro racial problems	199
20. Preserving states' rights	191
21. Strengthening the United Nations	190
22. The trend toward a more powerful Federal Government	181
23. Problems of labor and labor-management relations	177

a Concern about maintaining law and order may have been somewhat inflated because the racial riots during the summer of 1964 were still fresh in the public mind at the time of the interviews.

b Concern about Vietnam undoubtedly rose later as the American military effort escalated.

cerned about a number of sweeping international problems; that, next, they are concerned about certain substantive domestic problems and programs; and that they are bothered least of all by ideological issues. Particularly noteworthy is the fact that concern about "government spending" was in eighteenth place and concern about "the trend toward a more powerful Federal Government" in the next to last position.

Operational vs. Ideological Concerns

In order to get a picture of the way concerns were patterned, overall average scores were calculated in three broad areas. A grouping of the international items in Table V-1 provided an average for *International Concerns;* the items dealing with education, Medicare, unemployment, and poverty formed the basis of an average score for *Operational Concerns;* and, finally, the items concerning individual liberties, free enterprise, the trend toward a more powerful Federal Government, and the preservation of states' rights were combined to give an average score for *Ideological Concerns.* Here are the comparative results:

International Concerns   231
Operational Concerns   217
Ideological Concerns   197

Among half the sample population (49 per cent), the average score for Operational Concerns was higher than that for Ideological; among 25 per cent it was the same; and the score for Ideological Concerns was higher than that for Operational among only 26 per cent.

Liberals vs. Conservatives

As would be expected, the priority of concerns among liberals in general tended to be operationally or prag-

matically oriented; among conservatives abstractly or ideologically oriented. As Table V-2 shows, the great majority of
complete liberals on the Operational Spectrum rated Operational Concerns higher than Ideological, while most of the
complete conservatives gave priority to the Ideological. In
related vein, three-fifths of those who said the Government
has too much power scored Ideological Concerns higher
than Operational. On the other hand, considerably more
than half of those who thought the Government has the
right amount of power and two-thirds of those who said it
should use its powers even more vigorously rated Operational Concerns higher.

TABLE V-2

OPERATIONAL *vs.* IDEOLOGICAL CONCERNS BY OPERATIONAL SPECTRUM

	Oper. Concerns Higher	Same	Ideol. Concerns Higher
Qualified on Operational Spectrum As			
Completely liberal	69%	24%	7%
Predominantly liberal	51	28	21
Middle of the road	34	30	36
Predominantly conservative	16	15	69
Completely conservative	6	8	86

Table V-3 shows the differences between operational
liberals and operational conservatives in greater detail,
giving the average scores for people in the various groups of
the Operational Spectrum on each item having to do with
Operational or Ideological Concerns. At every step from
complete liberal to complete conservative (with one minor
exception), the degree of concern for each item under
Operational Concerns decreases, while under Ideological
Concerns the degree of concern increases at every step.

Furthermore, among those who qualified as complete liberals, every single operational item was of greater concern than any one of the ideological items. Conversely, among those who were rated either predominantly or completely conservative, the degree of concern for every single ideological item was greater than for any one of the operational items.

Table V-3

Individual Concerns by Operational Spectrum

	Compl. Lib.	Pred. Lib.	Middle Road	Pred. Cons.	Compl. Cons.
Operational Concerns					
Improving our educational system	240	236	218	203	209
Unemployment in the U.S.	240	233	205	172	155
Reducing poverty in this country	244	221	197	162	136
Medicare for the elderly	237	206	189	154	144
Average score for all operational items	240	224	202	173	161
Ideological Concerns					
Preserving our free enterprise system	201	212	228	237	257
Preserving our individual liberties against government interference	185	201	218	255	279
Preserving states' rights	169	186	204	232	260
The trend toward a more powerful Federal Government	161	177	185	230	263
Average score for all ideological items	179	194	209	238	265

The implications are obvious. Those who qualified as liberal because they approved of crucial Federal programs involved in the Operational Spectrum did so because they were highly concerned about problems having to do with human needs which, to them, seemed to require Federal solutions; they were not inhibited in supporting these programs by the traditional American ideology. In the case of those who were rated conservative on our Operational Spectrum because they opposed such Federal programs, it would have been theoretically possible for them to be equally concerned about the problems but to feel that solutions such as state, local, or private, rather than Federal, were called for. This was not the situation, however. Rather, the conservatives not only gave priority to ideological considerations inhibiting Federal action, but actually across the board showed little concern for the actual operational problems. In short, in the conservatives' scheme of priorities, problems having to do with human needs were subordinated to considerations of principle and ideology.

Population Subgroups

The relative priority accorded Operational *vs.* Ideological Concerns helps to explain some of the group patterns described in earlier chapters on our various measurements of liberalism and conservatism. The proportion of people scoring Operational Concerns higher than Ideological * was very much larger among the less well educated, the poor, the workers, those living in big cities, and especially Negroes. People in all these groups are obviously close to the problems included in the score for Operational Concerns and feel Governmental assistance is essential to help them cope with problems which to them are real, not academic.

* The figures are given in Table 5 in Appendix F, pp. 225 f.

On the other hand, the proportions placing Ideological Concerns above Operational were highest among the college-educated, the well-to-do, the professional and business class, and people living in towns and rural areas. These people are of course less subject to, and hence less concerned about, the operational problems facing less fortunate groups and can better afford to subordinate these problems to traditional ideological considerations. In short, hostility to the Government and a high degree of concern for ideological issues, sufficient to inhibit the desire for Governmental assistance in meeting human needs, is a luxury that only a minority of the population feels it can indulge in. For the majority, when traditional ideology and operational needs conflict, the ideological is subordinated to the operational. This is why so many Americans give lip service to traditional conservative ideology but turn out to be liberals at the operational level of Government programs. In many cases, however, the conflict between ideological and operational orientations must lead to moments of ambivalence and bewilderment.

International Concerns

It was shown above that the American public as a whole expresses more concern about international than about domestic matters, a complete reversal from the situation that prevailed before World War II. In Table V-1, which listed in rank order the degree of concern about twenty-three problems and issues, it will be noted that the subjects of an international nature which topped the list constitute sweeping generalizations: keeping the country out of war, combatting world Communism, keeping our military defense strong, controlling the use of nuclear weapons, maintaining respect for the United States in other countries. Of less concern were such specifics as relations with Russia,

Communist China, Vietnam (our survey was conducted while the war in Vietnam was still at low pitch), keeping NATO and our other alliances strong, and strengthening the United Nations. From all this, it may be inferred that most people are more interested in and concerned about the grand objectives of foreign policy than about its mechanics or specific situations, about which they are not well informed, as we shall see in the next chapter.

Demographically, as would be expected, the average scores for International Concerns were lower among those with only a grade school education and the poor. However, even among the poorly educated, the score was 219 out of a possible 300, and among those with incomes of less than $3,000 it was 217, showing how deeply Americans at all levels are concerned with international matters. Regionally, the highest degree of concern was expressed in the East and West (236 and 237, respectively), with the lowest (219) in the Southern states that went for Goldwater in 1964. The Midwest—traditional home of isolationism—was in between (227), the same as the Southern states that gave President Johnson a majority. In general, however, all sections and all groups in the United States exhibited a deep concern about foreign affairs.

This may be in part because international problems seem more insoluble than those at home and hence give more cause for worry. But, basically, it is because almost all Americans have come to realize that international developments can, do, and will profoundly affect their own lives.

VI

International Outlooks

Ignorance About International Matters

Despite their high degree of concern about foreign policy problems, a surprising number of Americans are abysmally ignorant of the specifics of international affairs, even at the most elementary level. For example, a study conducted by the Survey Research Center of the University of Michigan for the Council on Foreign Relations in the late spring of 1964 [7] showed that one-fourth of the American people were not even aware that mainland China was ruled by a Communist Government. The same study revealed that, as of then, about one-fourth of those interviewed had not heard anything about the fighting in Vietnam. Although this was long before the big build-up there, the United States had been involved in that unhappy land for ten years and had advanced millions of dollars in aid and military assistance; there was a United States military mission of about sixteen thousand men in Vietnam; and news of Vietnam was headlined in newspapers and on television and radio almost every day. In a Gallup Poll taken at about the same time, almost two-thirds of the American public said they had paid little

59

or no attention to developments in South Vietnam (May 27, 1964).

As already mentioned, our own survey included a battery of questions testing information and knowledge on both domestic and international matters. On the international side, those interviewed were first asked to identify a number of prominent figures in world affairs whose names had figured in the news time after time. Considerable leeway was allowed in rating an answer as correct. For example, a reply that Ludwig Erhard was a German leader was accepted even though he was not specifically designated as the then Chancellor of West Germany. Even making these allowances, here are the percentages of people able to identify correctly four individuals, namely:

Charles de Gaulle	71%
U Thant	40
Ludwig Erhard	36
Sukarno	14

Another series of knowledge questions dealt with NATO, one of the keystones of American foreign policy. From these, it turned out that more than one-fourth of the American people (28 per cent) had never heard or read "of the North Atlantic Treaty Organization—NATO, that is." Only 58 per cent knew that the United States was a member of NATO and only 38 per cent that Russia was not a member. To be ignorant of these facts is obviously to be ignorant of the essential nature and purposes of the Atlantic Alliance. Also, only 21 per cent could say that neutral Sweden is not a member.

To simplify analysis, these eight items (identification of four international figures plus four questions about NATO) were used to rate respondents on an International Information Score, with the following overall results:

Well informed (6 to 8 correct)	26%
Moderately informed (3 to 5 correct)	35
Uninformed (0 to 2 correct)	39
	100%

In short, two-fifths of the American public appear to have too little information about international matters to play an intelligent role as citizens of a nation that is the world's leader, and only one-fourth are really adequately informed. Men tended to be better informed than women, and urban residents than rural. Older people were appreciably more ignorant than the young and the middle-aged. Regionally, Easterners and Westerners were the best informed, with Southerners the least, one-half of them falling into the "uninformed" category. And, of course, knowledge was highly stratified by income. The most dramatic variations were on the basis of education, as can be seen in Table VI-1. The difference between those with high school training and those with at least some college education is spectacular. It is interesting to note that veterans, many of whom have had experience abroad during their period of service, rated very much higher than non-veterans on the International Information Score.

TABLE VI-1
INTERNATIONAL INFORMATION SCORE BY EDUCATION

	Grade School	High School	College
Well informed	9%	25%	57%
Moderately informed	26	43	32
Uninformed	65	32	11
	100%	100%	100%

Internationalism vs. *Isolationism*

It must be hard for Americans not of the older generation to realize how extremely isolationist and neutralistic the United States was before World War II. The following questions, all drawn from Gallup Polls of that period, are indicative of the mood of the times:

QUESTION: Would you like to see the United States join the League of Nations? (October 18, 1937.)

Yes	33%
No	67

QUESTION: Which of these foreign policies should our Government follow: do everything possible to prevent war between foreign governments, even if it means threatening to fight countries which start wars, or do everything possible to keep us out of foreign wars? (March 10, 1937.)

Prevent war	6%
Keep us out of war	94

QUESTION: Should the United States and Great Britain make an agreement to use their armies and navies together to maintain world peace? (February 14, 1938.)

Yes	39%
No	50
No opinion	11

QUESTION: If one foreign nation insists upon attacking another, should the U.S. join with other nations to compel it to stop? (November 17, 1936.)

Yes	29%
No	71

QUESTION: Do you think it was a mistake for the United States to enter World War I? (April 4, 1937.)

Yes	70%
No	30

QUESTION: If another war like World War I developed in Europe, should America take part again? (February 14, 1937.)

Yes	5%
No	95

QUESTION: If Germany and Italy go to war against England and France, would it be better for the U.S. to help England and France or not help either side? (February 16, 1939.)

Help	30%
Not help	66
No opinion	4

In our fall of 1964 survey, the results on the following series of questions show how far Americans had come since those pre-World War II days of isolationism and neutralism:

QUESTION: Now, some more questions on international matters. First, please read all of the statements on this card; and then I'm going to ask you to tell me whether you agree or disagree with each of them.

How about the first statement: The United States should cooperate fully with the United Nations. Do you agree or disagree? *

Agree	72%
Disagree	16
Don't know	12
	100%

* Similarly, Gallup found that 83 per cent of the public thought it was very important to try to make the United Nations a success (February 4, 1962) and that 59 per cent felt there would likely have been another world war if the United Nations had not been in existence (June 25, 1965).

In deciding on its foreign policies, the United States should take into account the views of its Allies in order to keep our alliances strong.

Agree	81%
Disagree	7
Don't know	12
	100%

Since the United States is the most powerful nation in the world, we should go our own way in international matters, not worrying too much about whether other countries agree with us or not.

Agree	19%
Disagree	70
Don't know	11
	100%

The United States should mind its own business internationally and let other countries get along as best they can on their own.

Agree	18%
Disagree	70
Don't know	12
	100%

We shouldn't think so much in *international* terms but concentrate more on our own *national* problems and building up our strength and prosperity here at home.

Agree	55%
Disagree	32
Don't know	13
	100%

Apart from the last question, about which more will be said later, overwhelming majorities opted for the "internationalist" point of view.

International Patterns

In order to test internationalist and isolationist orientations on a generalized basis, a system of International Patterns was devised. To qualify as "completely internationalist" in this scheme, a respondent had to agree that the United States should cooperate fully with the United Nations and take into account the views of our Allies, and disagree with the statements that the United States should go its own way, mind its own business, and concentrate more on national problems. To be considered "completely isolationist," a respondent had to give exactly contrary answers. Categories were also provided for "predominantly internationalist" (meaning the individual followed a "completely internationalist" pattern in most but not all respects); "predominantly isolationist" (meaning he conformed to the "completely isolationist" pattern in most but not all respects); and a middle category labelled "mixed" (meaning there was a mixture of the internationalist and isolationist patterns).* The proportion of respondents in each category follows:

Completely internationalist	30%	⎫ 65%
Predominantly internationalist	35	⎭
Mixed	27	} 27
Predominantly isolationist	5	⎫ 8
Completely isolationist	3	⎭
	100%	

Thus, two decades after the end of World War II, the isolationists in this country were a small minority. Comments typical of the internationalist majority were as follows:

* A more complete, technical explanation of these procedures is given in Appendix E, pp. 211 ff.

My hope is that we will continue to consider other countries, not just ourselves. It's not just the U.S. anymore, but one world. (A miner in Arizona.)

We must integrate our activities with the world, because if we don't we all suffer. (An education specialist living in Massachusetts.)

I would like to see all the world set down to breakfast together with peace. (A male high school teacher in Oregon.)

Just so we don't stand alone. (The wife of a Chicago salesman.)

The worst possible view of the future is of Americans feeling superior to others in the world; that is, to be isolationists again. We could fail to achieve greatness. (The wife of a chef in a Maryland restaurant.)

On the other hand, the outlook of the isolationist minority was well summed up by an unemployed man living in Oregon:

Bring our boys back home and mind our own business. Don't interfere in other countries. Don't dominate the world but keep up our military strength. . . . We have spread ourselves out in so many countries it isn't good for us.

Population Subgroups

In terms of occupation, the professional and business groups were the most internationalist; the white-collar workers were the next.* Older people were less internationalist than younger. Internationalism was highly graduated by income, the well-to-do being very internationalist and the poor much less so. Correspondingly, the college-educated were substantially more internationalist than people with less edu-

* The figures are given in Table 6 in Appendix F, pp. 227 f.

cation. In related fashion, those who showed themselves well informed on our International Information Score were most heavily internationalist, the uninformed the least. Clearly, knowledge and better education create broader horizons and perspectives and provide a matrix for an internationalist outlook. The Midwest has outgrown its isolationism: it is now almost as international-minded as the East and more so than the West. The Southern states that went to Johnson in 1964 were at just about the national average, but the Southern states that gave Goldwater a majority were the least internationalist of any section of the country. The majority of all groups, nevertheless, proved to be internationalist.

Discussion of party, religious, and ethnic differences as they relate to domestic matters will be considered in Chapter IX, "Political Identifications." But here it can be noted that Republicans proved to be somewhat less internationalist than Democrats or Independents, although the differences between them were not marked; and that Roman Catholics were more internationalist than Protestants, and Jews more than Catholics, with eight out of ten Jews qualifying as internationalist.

Liberalism, Conservatism, and International Patterns

Since the percentage of isolationists was so small, it would make little sense to speak of conservatives as tending more toward isolationism than liberals. However, in each of the categories of liberalism and conservatism used, it turned out that conservatives were less internationalist than liberals. Table VI-2 gives the combined percentages of those who qualified as either completely or predominantly internationalist. While in every case the percentage of conservatives who were predominantly or completely internationalist was much lower than among the liberals, it must be noted that the internationalist pattern in this country today is so dominant that even half or more of the conservatives qualified as "internationalist," with the rest being chiefly in the "mixed" rather than the "isolationist" category. Still the relationship of liberalism and conservatism to internationalism is significant.[8]

TABLE VI-2

PER CENT INTERNATIONALIST OF LIBERALS AND CONSERVATIVES

	Internationalist
Those who qualified on the Operational Spectrum as	
Completely liberal	71%
Predominantly liberal	66
Middle of the road	63
Predominantly conservative	58
Completely conservative	50
Those who qualified on the Ideological Spectrum as	
Completely or predominantly liberal	76%
Middle of the road	71
Predominantly conservative	67
Completely conservative	51
Those who identified themselves as	
Liberal	73%
Middle of the road	69
Conservative	57

Trust in People

An interesting sidelight on the outlook of internationalists as compared with that of isolationists is that the former tend to have much more trust in their fellow human beings. Our survey included this question:

QUESTION: Some people say that human nature is basically bad and that you can't be too careful in your dealings with people. Others say that human nature is basically good and that people can be trusted. From your own experience, do you think human nature is basically good or basically bad?

As Table VI-3 shows, while the great majority of internationalists thought human nature is good and people can be trusted, only four out of ten of the isolationists agreed, with the majority feeling that human nature is either bad, or both good and bad, and that you have to be wary in dealing with people.

TABLE VI-3

HUMAN NATURE BY INTERNATIONAL PATTERNS

	Total Sample	Compl. Int'l	Predom. Int'l	Mixed	Isol.
Human nature is					
Good	67%	79%	71%	64%	39%
Bad	6	3	7	6	12
Both good and bad	25	17	21	29	46
Don't know	2	1	1	1	3
	100%	100%	100%	100%	100%

International Cooperation

When the Gallup Poll (July 3, 1963) asked whether it would be "better for the United States to keep independent in world affairs . . . or to work closely with other nations," more than eight out of ten of the public favored international cooperation. To find out with which countries the people thought the United States should cooperate, our own survey included this question:

QUESTION: Under present circumstances, which countries of
the world do you think it most important for the United
States to cooperate with *very closely?* Just name them
off as they come to mind.

The results are given in Table VI-4, arranged on a regional
basis. Clearly, the ideas Americans hold about international
cooperation are oriented chiefly toward Western Europe,
particularly Great Britain; secondly, toward the Western
Hemisphere; and, thirdly, toward Asia. Africa and the
Middle East get scant attention. The most surprising aspect
of these results is the 35 per cent who said the United States
should cooperate very closely with the Soviet Union and the
16 per cent who mentioned Communist China. Presumably
these people saw cooperation as an antidote to continuing
conflict and possible war. By way of example, a machinist
in Los Angeles named only Russia and China as countries
with which we should cooperate saying, "I think if an agreement could be reached between the three of us, nothing else
would be important." Similarly a fire insurance engineer
living in Massachusetts put the matter this way: "I want a
better agreement with other countries like Russia and China
so that the American people may live peacefully."

Most pertinent in showing the extent to which the American people have become international-minded is the fact
that only one per cent volunteered the answer that the
United States should not cooperate with any other nations,
and only 12 per cent were unable to name at least one country with which we should cooperate. There was a variation
on this theme in the case of one woman however (the wife
of a civil service employee in New York City), whose reaction to our question was this: "The other countries should
cooperate with us. We shouldn't cooperate with them."

TABLE VI-4

COUNTRIES WITH WHICH U.S. SHOULD COOPERATE

Europe

Great Britain; the British Commonwealth	54%
France	36
West Germany	27
Other specified Western European countries or Western Europe in general	15
Russia	35
East European satellites	1

Western Hemisphere

Canada	18
Cuba	3
Mexico	9
Other specified Latin-American countries or Western Hemisphere or Latin-American countries in general	19

Asia

Japan	14
Nationalist China	2
Communist China	16
Other specified Asian countries or Asia in general	9

Africa

Specified African countries or Africa in general	3

Middle East

Specified Middle Eastern countries or Middle East in general	2

Other

Miscellaneous countries or references (such as "the Free World," "our allies")	17
No countries in particular; U.S. shouldn't cooperate with any	1
Don't know; no answer	12

Foreign Aid

The internationalism of the American public is not quite as thoroughgoing as our story up to this point would indicate, however. An example is the less than complete enthusiasm shown by the people for one of the keystones of United States internationalism—foreign aid. A Gallup Poll release of March 13, 1966, reported these results:

QUESTION: In general, how do you feel about foreign aid— are you for it, or against it?

For it	53%
Against it	35
No opinion	12
	100%

The thrust of these figures had remained about the same in successive Gallup surveys since 1958. But in our own study, when the pocketbook aspect of this issue was explicitly mentioned, a different picture emerged:

QUESTION: And, now, what about economic aid to foreign countries? Do you think Government spending for this purpose should be kept at least at the present level, or reduced, or ended altogether?

Present level or increased	32%
Reduced	44
Ended	15
Don't know	9
	100%

In short, when the question of foreign aid was presented in the context of Government spending, six out of ten opted for reduction, if not termination. Typical comments on this matter were as follows:

I worry that we have too much of a "give-away" policy. I think we should take care of our own first. Otherwise the rest of the world will walk all over us. (A teacher in California.)

So many people are out of jobs here and the country is helping other countries. . . . Our own people should be helped before foreign countries. (A Negro living in Detroit.)

I don't want the taxpayers of the U.S. to feed the rest of the world forever. We could go broke. (An executive of an automobile firm in Texas.)

The U.S. is trying to buy the friendship of other countries. It just can't be done. (A Tennessee salesman.)

We have helped other countries but they don't appreciate it. (A widow in Wisconsin.)

Well, I think they still think of us as Uncle Sucker. (A maintenance chief for an electric company in California.)

Sentiment in favor of terminating or reducing rather than continuing economic assistance at the current level predominated in all population subgroups, but was especially strong among people over fifty, among those living in smaller cities and towns and in rural areas, among Southerners and Westerners, and particularly among the Republicans and, as might be expected, the conservatives. While the college-educated and well-to-do were in general more internationalist than the rest of the population, they were only slightly more in favor of continuation of foreign aid at the current level. It was only among those who qualified as "complete internationalists" that continuation of foreign aid was favored by a slim majority. And when those classified as "predominantly internationalist" are added to the "complete internationalists," the majority in favor of continued foreign aid evaporates.

Thus, the internationalism of Americans is qualified by their attitudes toward foreign aid. The reason for this, of course, is that such aid involves Government spending for objectives that many Americans do not relate directly to their own purposes. Concern about Government spending in general varied greatly according to the alternative chosen in our foreign aid question. Out of a maximum score of 300, those who favored maintaining or increasing the present level of foreign aid rated their concern about Government spending in general at 180, those who advocated a reduction in foreign aid at 219, and those who opted for termination at 235.

Kinds of Aid and Political Strings

The generally negative picture seen so far is not all that those concerned with public support for foreign aid programs need worry about. The Gallup Poll mentioned at the beginning of this section, which showed the public in favor of foreign aid in principle, also contained this question:

QUESTION: Which, if any, of the kinds of foreign aid listed on this card do you favor? Name as many or as few as you favor.

1. Train teachers, build schools, provide books   65%
2. Help improve farming methods, provide farm equipment   61
3. Build hospitals, train nurses and doctors, provide medicines   61
4. Provide birth control information   43
5. Send surplus food   41
6. Help build factories and industries   33
7. Build highways and railroads   21
8. Help build up military strength   18
None   4
No opinion   8

Clearly, most support for foreign aid seems to gravitate toward activities which might be called humanitarian, such as education and health. There appears to be little understanding of or support for those aspects having to do with economic development, such as helping to build factories and industries, highways and railroads. Yet, in terms of the long-range improvement of the lives of people in underdeveloped areas, economic development is the heart of the matter.

Perhaps most distressing of all to those who advocate foreign aid without political strings, the same Gallup release of March 13, 1966, reported these results:

QUESTION: Suppose another country—which is receiving foreign aid from the United States—fails to support the United States in a major foreign policy decision, such as Vietnam. Do you think the United States should continue giving aid to that country, reduce aid, or cut off aid completely?

Continue aid	16%
Reduce aid	30
Cut off completely	45
No opinion	9
	100%

Thus, in the eyes of a majority of the public, although foreign aid is primarily a humanitarian endeavor on the part of America, it should nevertheless be repaid by political support for the United States on the international scene.

Higher Priority for National Problems

Another qualification to the internationalism of Americans has already been mentioned. Despite the greater concern they registered for international than for domestic affairs, a majority of Americans nonetheless felt it was more important to solve the problems here at home than those at the international level. It will be recalled that more than half of our sample population agreed with the following statement, with only one-third disagreeing: "We shouldn't think so much in international terms but concentrate more on our own national problems and building up our strength and prosperity here at home." It was their agreement with this statement which prevented most of those who scored *"predominantly* internationalist" on the system of International Patterns from qualifying as *"completely* internationalist." Our feeling was that, even if a person favors international cooperation, he should not be classified as a complete internationalist so long as he gives a higher priority to national problems than to international.

There was not much difference between Republicans and Democrats in their reactions to the statement. The belief that we should concentrate more on national problems was commoner among people fifty years of age or over, the poorly educated, those with family incomes of under $5,000 a year, and people living in smaller towns and rural areas. Although to a lesser extent, the same belief was also prevalent among the young, the middle-income group, and people living in the larger cities. In only two closely related segments of the population was there a majority disagreeing with the statement: those with a college education and the well-to-do. Apparently the wider horizons and perspectives of these groups have sensitized them to the fact that at this point in history international problems cannot be subordinated to national. A wealthy farm owner and political leader in Maryland put his finger on the nub of the matter: "Given a hundred years, I believe we'll solve *all* of our internal problems. But we can't solve any of them if we can't stay both alive and free. If we don't concentrate on the international questions, we're doomed."

The attitude that we should concentrate more on national than on international problems was reflected, in a sense, in a poll Gallup took for us in January 1966:

QUESTION: In his recent State of the Union speech to Congress, the President said that, despite the cost of the war in Vietnam, the Administration would continue its programs for Federal aid to education, medical care, cleaning up water pollution, the war against poverty and other Great Society programs. How do you feel about this—do you think the Government should continue to pay for these programs here at home, or do you feel they should be cut back to help finance the war in Vietnam?

Should continue	58%
Should cut back	25
Other	7
No opinion	10
	100%

We have seen that two-thirds of the American people qualified as internationalist on our system of International Patterns because they believed in international cooperation by the United States. Yet the fact that a majority felt we should concentrate more on national than on international problems raises a definite question of whether American internationalism is really as deeply ingrained as some of the findings imply. The outlook of most Americans seems best described as one of qualified internationalism.

Image of the United States Abroad

While the internationalism of Americans may be qualified and a majority may feel we should concentrate more on national problems, as a people we are still very sensitive to the image of America held by people abroad. It will be recalled that in Table V-1 in the chapter on "The Concerns of Americans," the item "maintaining respect for the United States in other countries" held fifth place in the order of concerns. This high degree of involvement about maintaining respect for the United States is illustrative of what former Secretary of State Dean Acheson meant when he said that Americans have a "Narcissus psychosis": "An American is apt to stare like Narcissus at his image in the pool of what he believes to be world opinion." [9] Quite obviously, Americans want to be loved, but, if they can't be loved, they certainly want to be respected.

At the time of our survey, half of the public thought respect for the United States was high abroad but a large minority disagreed:

QUESTION: Now, let's think of the image—or picture—that people in other countries have of the United States. From what you have heard or read, do you think United States prestige abroad is high or low at the present time?

High	52%
Low	39
Don't know	9
	100%

There were significant differences in the results when scaled according to our International Information Score: the well informed held a jaundiced view, the moderately informed were sanguine, while the uninformed were positively euphoric. Similarly, the response of the majority of college-educated people was negative; of those with only a high school or grade school education, positive. Apparently, the more one knows about international affairs, the less well he thinks the United States is doing abroad. The reader will have to decide for himself whether this is realism or pessimism.

The Dominican Republic, Cuba, and Vietnam

As shown in Table V-1, p. 52, next to keeping the country out of war, combatting world Communism is the greatest concern of the American public. And there is little doubt that many American attitudes and reactions to the international scene are motivated by strong feelings of anti-Communism. One of the questions that arises, of course, is how far the public is willing to go in combatting Communism in conflict situations.

So far as the Western Hemisphere is concerned, Harris found that almost eight out of ten Americans thought it was right for the United States to use military power to keep Communists out of North and South America (July 5, 1965). In the same release he reported that a somewhat higher proportion approved President Johnson's sending United States Marines into the Dominican Republic to protect Americans there and that three-fourths of the public agreed with the President on "increasing U.S. troops to 22,000 to keep the Communists from taking over."

In the wake of the ill-fated Bay of Pigs invasion, Gallup found that two-thirds of the public were against sending our armed forces into Cuba to help overthrow Castro; that opinion was about equally divided on the question of aiding the anti-Castro forces with money and war materials; but that two-thirds thought the United States should refuse to buy from or sell to Cuba so long as Castro was in power (May 7, 1961). In our own survey in the fall of 1964, we asked this question:

QUESTION: Some people say the United States should use stronger measures in dealing with the Cuban problem, including a naval blockade to stop supplies from going into Cuba, or from Cuba to other countries for purposes of subversion. Other people say such measures are unnecessary and would be dangerous because they would risk a major war. How do you feel about this—would you favor or oppose stronger measures, including a naval blockade, under present circumstances?

Favor	47%
Oppose	34
Don't know	19
	100%

Democrats were about equally divided on this question, but Republicans favored stronger measures by a ratio of more than two to one. More in favor than other segments of the population were people fifty years of age and over, the upper income groups, people living in the West, and those in small towns and rural areas. Since these groups tend to be more on the conservative side, it is no surprise that, while the complete liberals on the Operational Spectrum were about equally divided, the conservatives were overwhelmingly in favor of stronger measures. On the basis of our system of International Patterns, only the complete internationalists were preponderantly opposed to stronger measures by a modest margin; the majority of even the predominant internationalists, as well as of the mixed group and the isolationists, were in favor.

Another conflict situation asked about in our survey was Vietnam. The interviewing took place in late September and early October 1964. This was after the retaliatory bombing of North Vietnam following a PT boat attack on United States destroyers in the Bay of Tonkin, but prior to the beginning of major air strikes against North Vietnam and other forms of escalation in early 1965. Since a major issue in the campaign of 1964 was whether or not to step up the war in Vietnam, our results are of historical interest in showing the degree of belligerency then advocated by the American public:

QUESTION: In general, are you satisfied or dissatisfied with the way the United States Government is handling the problem of Vietnam?

Very satisfied	7%	} 37%
Somewhat satisfied	30	
Somewhat dissatisfied	23	} 40%
Very dissatisfied	17	
Don't know	23	
	100%	

QUESTION: There would seem to be three basic courses the United States could follow in Vietnam. On balance which one of these [listed on a card] would you favor?

1. Pull out entirely. 16%
2. Keep on about the way we have been. 37
3. Step up the war by carrying the fighting to North Vietnam, for example through more air strikes against Communist territory. 29
Don't know 18
100%

Thus, only a minority wanted to pull out of Vietnam, with the dominant sentiment being to go on "as is," and a sizeable proportion advocating that the war be stepped up. A retired letter carrier in Texas probably expressed the underlying feeling of many, however, when he said: "We've got a bear by the tail in Vietnam and don't know how to turn it loose."

For the most part, the pattern of responses to this question was substantially similar to the pattern in the poll on Cuba. Democrats were preponderantly in favor of keeping on as we were; Republicans leaned toward stepping up the war. The lower and middle income groups and those with only a grade or high school education were preponderantly for the "as is" alternative; the well-to-do by a narrow margin and the college-educated by a majority were for stepping up the war. The liberals leaned toward "as is"; the conservatives toward "step up." Regionally, the highest degree of sentiment for stepping up the war was found in the West.

There were two interesting differences in responses to the Cuba and Vietnam questions. In the first place, while older people were most in favor of stronger measures against Cuba, it was the young who were most heavily in favor of stepping up the war in Vietnam, despite the fact that their age group would have to do most of the fighting. The second difference has to do with our system of International Patterns. Internationalists, as might be expected, were definitely in favor of continuing as we were. On the other hand, while a majority of the small band of isolationists advocated stronger measures against Cuba, they were predominantly in favor of pulling out of Vietnam. Apparently, in their eyes, there was a difference between a conflict with Communism in nearby Cuba and one in far-off Vietnam. Nor was this sentiment limited to isolationists: half of those who were for pulling out of Vietnam nevertheless favored stronger measures against Cuba.

Taking both questions into account, the results show that those who were for stronger measures against Cuba and for stepping up the war in Vietnam (the "hawks") made up one-third of the total of those who expressed opinions on both questions, while only one-tenth opposed stronger measures against Cuba and advocated pulling out of Vietnam (the "doves").

Relations with Russia

On the surface the American public exhibits a certain amount of ambivalence concerning how best to deal with the Soviet Union. First of all, there is the belief that the United States should be firm. This is reflected in the reactions to one of the statements included in our survey:

STATEMENT: The United States should take a firmer stand against the Soviet Union than it has in recent years.

Agree	61%
Disagree	25
Don't know	14
	100%

The somewhat more extreme comments on this subject tended to run along the following lines:

Russia has always been a threat. In fact, we are surrounded by threats right now. I'd hate to see someone get in office who would back away, that is, compromise. I think we have to be firm in our decisions if we want to maintain peace. (The wife of a casket maker in Iowa.)

My hope is that the U.S. will put a firm step down on the Communist nations. And, instead of letting them get away with what they have in the past, don't stop at half-way measures. Go all out and finish it even if it means war. Then, maybe, we can get the nations to live together in peace. (A millwright living in Michigan.)

I'd like to see them have a showdown with Russia and Red China and see where we stand. I think they're pulling the wool over our eyes and fooling our statesmen. (A Government clerk in Maryland.)

Things will get pretty bad if a line is not drawn somewhere with regard to Russia. (A truck driver living in Brooklyn, New York.)

As might be expected, Republicans and conservatives agreed that we should be firmer with much greater frequency than did Democrats and liberals. However, among all the groups we have been discussing—including the complete internationalists—a majority favored a firmer stand vis-à-vis Russia.

At the same time, a majority of the public did not accept the contention of the extreme right that our Government was appeasing the Communists:

STATEMENT: President Johnson and his Administration have been following a defeatist "no win" policy on the international front by appeasing the Communists.

Agree	27%
Disagree	52
Don't know	21
	100%

In acting with firmness toward Russia, the American people did not advocate going so far as to try to roll back the Iron Curtain:

STATEMENT: The United States should seek to roll back the Iron Curtain and liberate the satellite countries from Soviet control, even if this might provoke Russia to go to war.

Agree	20%
Disagree	59
Don't know	21
	100%

One reason for this cautious attitude of the majority is, no doubt, that most Americans do not accept the idea that the Soviet Union would not fight, if faced with strong provocation.

STATEMENT: No matter what the United States does, the Russian leaders won't risk launching a nuclear war.

Agree	28%
Disagree	52
Don't know	20
	100%

While a substantial majority believed we should take a firmer stand against Russia, an overwhelming majority indicated a willingness to negotiate with the Soviet Union.

STATEMENT: The United States should continue to negotiate with the Soviet Union on a broad front in the hope of reaching agreements which would contribute to world peace.

Agree	85%
Disagree	7
Don't know	8
	100%

Even 80 per cent of those who said the United States should take a firmer stand against Russia were in favor of negotiating.

STATEMENT: In particular, the United States should continue to negotiate with Russia with a view toward reducing armaments on both sides.

Agree	70%
Disagree	19
Don't know	11
	100%

While liberals were much more in favor of this proposition, a majority of conservatives, as well as of Republicans, also agreed to continuing negotiations for the reduction of armaments.

In accordance with this general line of thinking, Gallup found that, at the time it was up for ratification, almost two-thirds of the public thought the Senate should vote approval of the nuclear test-ban treaty with Russia (September 1, 1963). Three years later, Harris reported that, in retrospect, three-fourths thought it was good that the United States had signed the treaty; and that two-thirds favored an additional treaty with Russia under which both countries would agree not to help other nations build atomic bombs— in other words, a non-proliferation pact (October 16, 1966). This willingness to negotiate about armaments even carries over to Communist China. In the middle of 1966, two-fifths of the populace felt, now that Communist China had the bomb, that we should try to negotiate an atomic test-ban treaty with the Chinese, as we have with the Russians, with only one-fifth opposed (Harris: June 27, 1966).

Thus, the general feeling seemed to be that we should be firm with the Russians but keep on talking. Apparently the American public cherishes the hope that if we go on talking, some sort of accommodation will take place and everything will turn out all right. This faith is fortified by the belief of three-fifths of the people that it is possible to reach a peaceful settlement of differences with Russia, while only one-fourth think it impossible (Gallup: December 4, 1964). One avenue for achieving better understanding is, apparently, thought to be greater trade. A majority (55 per cent) felt the United States and Russia should "work out a business arrangement to buy and sell more goods to each other," with only one-third taking the negative view (Gallup: October 25, 1963).

Communist China

Our interviewing was conducted some time before the talk about showing greater flexibility toward Red China came into vogue and before the phrase "containment but not isolation" became a catchword. We were therefore surprised to find that, even in the fall of 1964, the public was almost evenly divided as to whether the United States should eventually recognize Communist China:

QUESTION: Do you think it would be in the interests of the United States to establish diplomatic relations with Communist China within the next five years or not?

Would be	36%
Would not be	39
Don't know	25
	100%

Democrats were split in two on the Chinese issue while a large plurality of Republicans were opposed. Those who qualified as liberal on the Operational Spectrum were preponderantly in favor; conservatives were heavily opposed. A considerable plurality of complete internationalists were on the affirmative side; a majority of isolationists on the negative. The stratification by age was marked: almost half of those in the 21–29 age group adopted the positive position, as compared with only one-fourth of those fifty and over. By region, the East and Midwest leaned toward the affirmative; the South and West toward the negative.

Subsequently, in mid-1966, Harris found that a majority of the public favored recognition of China, but the wording of the question he used was somewhat weighted in that direction:

QUESTION: It has been argued that we could deal with Red China better if we recognized Communist China. This would allow us to have an ambassador in China as we have in other Communist countries. Do you favor or oppose recognition by the United States of Communist China? (June 27, 1966.)

Favor	57%
Oppose	43
	100%

At the same time, two-thirds thought we should continue our "defensive treaty alliance with Chiang Kai-shek and Nationalist China (Formosa)." When it came to United Nations membership, the same Harris study found that more than three-fifths opposed admitting Communist China, but when the question was asked the following way, a majority were in favor:

QUESTION: It has been suggested that both Communist China and Nationalist China (Formosa) be made members of the United Nations, as two different countries. Would you favor or oppose this as a solution? (June 27, 1966).

Favor	55%
Oppose	45
	100%

Gallup found that, while 56 per cent opposed admitting Red China into the United Nations (with only 25 per cent in favor) when the wording of the question was simply, "Do you think Communist China should or should not be admitted as a member of the United Nations?" the majority went the other way when the phraseology was as follows:

QUESTION: Would you favor the admission of Communist China if it would improve U.S. and Communist China relations? (October 9, 1966.)

Favor	55%
Oppose	30
No opinion	15
	100%

Thus American public opinion seems to be fairly malleable when it comes to the Chinese problem.[10]

At the same time, our survey showed that there is strong belief that Communist China constitutes more of a danger to the United States than does Russia:

QUESTION: Which do you think will turn out to be the greater threat to the United States—Soviet Russia or Communist China?

Russia	19%
China	54
Both	18
Don't know	9
	100%

Typical comments went along this line:

The thing or the nation I think the U.S. has to fear is China —even more so now that they have the atom bomb. I don't think the Chinese are responsible people. I think we have to fear the Chinese more than the Russians. Life is cheap over there. (A supervisor in an optical laboratory in New York City.)

My worry is if China decides to blast off that bomb they just got. I think Russia will hold off, but I am worried about China. The Chinese place no value on life. (The wife of a paymaster, also in New York City.)

My hope is for peace all over the world, including Russia. The Arabs and Jews being able to live peaceably. And Red China being bombed out. (Another New York woman.)

A salesman living in Texas, however, did not show such partiality:

My hope is for peace in the world—and, if not that, the complete destruction of both Russia and China.

Defense

Taking the Chinese and other threats into account, there
was solid support for a military program adequate to maintain America's security and position in the world:

QUESTION: Is it your impression that the strength of United
States defense is about right at present, or do you feel that
it should be either increased or decreased?

About right	52%
Increased	31
Decreased	4
Don't know	13
	100%

Our survey was undertaken after the Kennedy Administration had very significantly built up United States defensive
capacity, an expansion which was still proceeding under
President Johnson. Yet only 4 per cent of the public advocated any reduction in that program, despite its cost,
while 83 per cent supported at least the current level if not
an increase. One woman (the wife of a New York salesman)
went so far as to say that she would like to see the United
States "the leader of democracy *and the leader of the arms
race.*" Despite a desire for peace and a dread of nuclear
war, the American public is opposed to decreasing our military establishment, apparently because of a belief that peace
can be maintained only through deterrence and a balance
of terror:

War isn't a fear at all because we kick in so much for military upkeep. (The wife of a salesman in Chicago.)

I think Russia is just as afraid as we are to let off the bomb
and will curb it as long as we do. (A housewife in Florida.)

I don't think there will be any war. There may be skir-
mishes, but nothing big because the one that would start

trouble would suffer as much as the other. (A road engineer in the State of Washington.)

One of the reasons I'm for Goldwater is the fact that I'm in complete agreement with him that the only way to maintain peace is by remaining strong. And when people think you haven't the will to fight or the courage to fight, that there's going to be constant appeasement, then it's going to be another situation like Chamberlain and Munich. (A female Republican leader in California.)

At the end of 1964, eight out of ten Americans thought that another world war would be avoided if the United States remained strong militarily (Harris: December 28, 1964).

Status and Power

We have seen that the great majority of Americans believe in international cooperation and approve continuing negotiations with Russia to relax tensions and to reduce armaments. On the other hand, consistent with the belief that we should take a firmer stand against Russia and with our great concern about the respect due the United States in other countries is the importance assigned to maintaining the power, position, and leadership of the United States on the world scene. In the case of some respondents, this feeling carried messianic overtones:

It is my hope that the U.S. will be a leading example for freedom and peace and the rest of the world would copy. (A welder of Mexican birth living in Los Angeles.)

We will make more achievements toward the betterment of man. We will be setting a pace for other nations and will lead. (A carpenter in Pennsylvania.)

My aspiration is that we be an example and leader for the world—in freedom. An inspiration to others to "seek the good life." (A chemist in Illinois.)

I want the U.S. to continue to show the rest of the world how democracy works. We've got to do this or be lost. (A retired civil engineer in Tennessee.)

My wish is to improve the few things wrong with the U.S. and pattern the rest of the world after us. (A maintenance man in California.)

Others put greater stress on power, as such, either for its own sake or for the accomplishment of our purposes:

To keep on being the biggest nation in the world. To keep on leading. . . . That we remain at the top—the very best and looked-up-to nation in the world. (A Texas salesman.)

We must stay the most powerful. (A factory worker in Georgia.)

I'd like to see the U.S. Number One in the world as far as power and wisdom are concerned. (A housewife in Michigan.)

Stay on top so far as any other countries are concerned. In other words, ahead of Russia. (The wife of a painter in Michigan.)

I feel we should put foreign countries in their place. After all, we're supporting them and I feel we should get a little tough with them because, if we don't, they will start demanding more and more, and walk all over us. (The wife of a clothing store executive in Baltimore.)

I would wish the United States to keep on being a powerful nation so as to help keep peace in the world. (An automobile mechanic in Texas.)

To build up the power of the U.S. so that the world would not take advantage of us. (A bank officer in Wisconsin.)

The importance assigned to maintaining the power and position of the United States is reflected in reactions to an-

other of the statements which those interviewed were asked
to assess:

STATEMENT: The United States should maintain its dominant position as the world's most powerful nation at all
costs, even going to the very brink of war, if necessary.

Agree	56%
Disagree	31
Don't know	13
	100%

The proportions agreeing that the United States must maintain its dominant position at all costs were significantly
higher than average among men, Republicans, conservatives,
isolationists, those fifty years of age and over, the well-to-do,
and people living in the West, and in towns and rural areas
throughout the country. But even a majority of women,
Democrats, liberals, internationalists, the young, the poor,
and people living in large cities and in regions other than
the West also agreed.

This widespread acceptance of the proposition that America's dominant position should be maintained at all costs
can be taken as a national determination that the United
States should not allow itself to be pushed around. Potentially, at least, it might also be considered a reflection of
what Senator J. William Fulbright is warning against at the
present time: "the arrogance of power." At the very least,
it indicates there is a decidedly nationalistic flavor to the
international outlook of Americans.

VII

Aspirations and Fears

The Self-Anchoring Scale

In the story so far there have been inklings of the values underlying the political orientations of the American people. In order to pin down this relationship more solidly, we included in our survey what is called the Self-Anchoring Striving Scale.[11] This device enables an investigator to learn what a person's aspirations and fears are and makes quantification and comparison possible among population groups.

The technique involves asking a person to describe in his own words, on the basis of his own assumptions, perceptions, goals, and values, what he feels would be the best possible life for himself. At the other extreme, he is asked to define the worries and fears involved in his conception of the worst possible life. Thus he delineates the spectrum of values which he is concerned about and by means of which he evaluates his own life. Then, using a nonverbal ladder device, with the top being the best life as he has defined it, and the bottom the worst, he is asked where he thinks he stands on the ladder today. He is also asked where he thinks he stood in the past and then where he thinks he will stand in the future.

Similar questions are put to him about the best and worst possible situations he can imagine for his country, thus revealing the spectrum of values he brings to bear in judging the state of the nation. All replies are carefully coded by specially trained people according to a scheme that has proved highly reliable in a number of studies and contains 145 different categories.[12] The exact wording of the questions follows:

QUESTION: All of us want certain things out of life. When you think about what really matters in your own life, what are your wishes and hopes for the future? In other words, if you imagine your future in the *best* possible light, what would your life look like, if you are to be happy?

QUESTION: Now, taking the other side of the picture, what are your fears and worries about the future? In other words, if you imagine your future in the *worst* possible light, what would your life look like then?

QUESTION: [Hand respondent card showing ladder.] * Here is a ladder symbolic of the "ladder of life." Let's suppose the top of the ladder [pointing] represents the *best* possible life for you and the bottom [pointing] represents the *worst* possible life for you. On which step of the ladder [moving finger rapidly up and down ladder] do you feel you personally stand at the present time?

On which step would you say you stood five years ago?

Just as your best guess, on which step do you think you will be five years from now?

QUESTION: Now, what are your wishes and hopes for the future of the United States? If you picture the future of

* The card showed a picture of a ladder with steps numbered from ten at the top to zero at the bottom.

the United States in the *best* possible light, how would things look, let's say, about ten years from now?

QUESTION: And what about your fears and worries for the future of our country? If you picture the future of the United States in the *worst* possible light, how would things look about ten years from now?

QUESTION: Looking at the ladder again, suppose the top represents the *very best* situation for our country, the bottom, the *very worst* situation for our country. Please show me on which step of the ladder you think the United States is at the present time.

On which step would you say the United States was *five years ago*—that is, toward the end of the Eisenhower Administration?

Now, looking a decade ahead, just as your best guess, where do you think the United States will be on the ladder *ten years from now* if everything goes as you expect?

Personal Aspirations and Fears

The results on the first question concerning personal aspirations are given in Table VII-1 and on the second question concerning personal fears in Table VII-2. In both cases, items mentioned by less than 5 per cent of the total sample have been omitted for the sake of simplicity.

Even in affluent America, the leading item mentioned under personal wishes and hopes was an "improved or decent standard of living." As one Arizona housewife pointed out, "they say it's prosperous now, but I sure as heck don't notice it." Mostly this aspiration took the form of a desire for a modest improvement, as in the case of a security guard in Michigan:

Everybody wants the best out of life. I wouldn't want to be a millionaire, but I would like enough money to stand in

TABLE VII-1

PERSONAL ASPIRATIONS

(Specified by 5% or more of sample)

Improved or decent standard of living	40%
Children—adequate opportunities for them (particularly education); children themselves do well, be happy, successful	35
Own health	29
Health of family	25
Happy family life	18
Peace; no war or threat of war	17
Have own house or get better one	12
Maintain status quo	12
Emotional stability and maturity—peace of mind	9
Good job, congenial work	9
Employment	8
Happy old age	8
Resolution of one's own religious, spiritual or ethical problems	6
Recreation, travel, leisure time	5
Wealth	5

TABLE VII-2

PERSONAL FEARS

(Specified by 5% or more of sample)

War	29%
Health of family	27
Own health	25
Deterioration in or inadequate standard of living	19
Unemployment	14
Children—inadequate opportunities for them (particularly education); children themselves do poorly, be unhappy, unsuccessful	10
Can't think of any fears or worries	10
Relatives—separation from; not able to help or take care of them	8
Communism	8
To be dependent on others	6
Lack of freedom, including specifically freedom of speech, religion, etc.	6

my own shoes. I want more than the way I live now. I'd like a little more comfort and security. I'd like a better job without having to worry when I might get laid off. I'd like to live in a nice flat . . . I don't want to be like Liz Taylor, afraid to step outside because she's rich and popular. I just want enough money to live a little better without any worry.

But the ambitions of a few went much further, as in the case of an importer living in Texas:

I would like to be a millionaire. That is all that would make me happy. I have everything else I need.

Under the second most-often-mentioned personal aspiration (opportunities for one's children), a frequent refrain was stated by a widow who worked as a bookkeeper in Indiana: "My hope is to get my children through college. I have a son who graduated this year and I have two more to put through. If I can do that I'll be very happy." As a production planner in a California aircraft concern saw it, "If a man doesn't have an education, he's going to be out of it in the future." It was perhaps this assumption which caused one of those interviewed (a female clerical worker in Georgia) to put the matter this way: "I would wish that everyone could get all the education they want—and maybe more." Many of the remarks were indicative of the high expectations Americans hold for the efficacy of education:

A more educated people will make a better world. (The wife of a Missouri farmer who never finished high school.)

If we were better educated, we wouldn't have to worry about wars and racial problems. (A housewife in California.)

While a number of aspirations and fears listed in the two tables might have at least a potential relationship to political orientations, some are especially salient. These include aspirations and/or fears having to do with the respondent's personal economic or living conditions (primarily standard of living and secondarily housing), with employment or unemployment, with opportunities for his or her children, with political matters such as the fear of Communism or of loss of freedom, and with international subjects such as peace and war. The percentages of the total sample mentioning topics in each of these categories, either as a hope, as a fear, or both, are given in Table VII-3.

TABLE VII-3

SELECTED CATEGORIES OF PERSONAL HOPES AND FEARS

Personal economic or living conditions	56%
Employment or unemployment	19
Children—opportunities for, etc.	38
Political subjects	22
International matters	41

Since our questions were pitched specifically at the level of the respondent's own personal life, the fact that four out of ten volunteered an international item makes it apparent that preoccupation with the international field, chiefly peace and war, is part and parcel of the daily lives of many Americans. Many of the comments emphasized this fact:

I guess we always live in fear of war in this country. (A housewife in Wisconsin.)

There wouldn't be a United States if they ever hit us with an atom bomb. (The wife of an electric power company employee, also in Wisconsin.)

For one thing, I don't want no war. I don't want to be dead. (An unemployed carpenter in California.)

The fear of war. My husband is very eligible. (The wife of an engine plant supervisor in Michigan.)

I have three boys to go to war and it's bad. (A timber worker in Tennessee.)

I worry about my grandsons having to go to war. I've experienced sending my own boys. That was bad I mean to tell you. (An old woman living on social security in Tennessee.)

My husband is in the National Guard. If a war broke out, I would be in bad shape with four children. (The wife of an appliance repairman in Massachusetts.)

Table VII-4 shows the considerable differences in the frequency with which the noninternational categories related to political orientations are mentioned by people in various categories of the Operational Spectrum. The operational liberals were much more preoccupied with their personal or family situation than were the conservatives, while a much larger proportion of conservatives referred to political matters. The same tendencies are evident on the Ideological Spectrum and on the question about Government power, although the relationships are less marked. In short, the values liberals bring to bear in evaluating their own lives

TABLE VII-4
SELECTED PERSONAL HOPES AND FEARS OF LIBERALS AND CONSERVATIVES

	Personal Economic	Employment-Unemployment	Children	Political
Operational Spectrum				
Liberal	60%	22%	41%	18%
Middle of the road	52	17	35	26
Conservative	41	6	30	42

are such that they tend to be preoccupied with personal and family needs, a tendency that makes them receptive to Governmental actions to meet those needs. On the other hand, even at the personal level, the values of the conservatives extend more widely to considerations of a political or ideological nature which inhibit favorable responses toward such Governmental action.

Personal Ladder Ratings

The average ratings given by the sample population when asked to evaluate their personal lives on our "ladder of life" for the past, present, and future were as follows:

Past	5.96
Present	6.85
Future	7.89

Clearly, people had a sense of personal progress over the past few years and thought their lot would be even better in the future. It should be stressed that all ratings are obviously subjective, the central idea of the Self-Anchoring Striving Scale. The interviewee is asked to evaluate his life on the basis of his own particular spectrum of values, which may differ in kind or degree from those of others. These values are by no means necessarily confined to the economic aspects of life. An individual may be poor but happy, in which event, in theory at least, he should place himself on one of the top rungs of the ladder. In practice, however, on the average the poor gave themselves lower present ratings than did the better off. Exposed as we all are to television and other forms of mass communication, everyone these days is aware of what is potentially available and tends to judge his lot against that potential. Similarly, people with a grade school or high school education ranked themselves lower than those with a college education. The same was true of other groups found to lean more toward the liberal side: for example, the blue-collar workers, people living in large cities, and especially Negroes.* It thus comes as no surprise that operational liberals assigned themselves lower average ratings in the present than did conservatives, as can be seen in Table VII-5. The same tendency was evident on our Ideological Spectrum, as shown in Table 7 in Appendix F, p. 230. Also, on the question regarding Governmental power, the same table shows that those who thought the Government should use its powers even more vigorously gave themselves the lowest average rating, and those who felt the Government had too much power the highest rating.

TABLE VII-5

PERSONAL LADDER RATINGS BY OPERATIONAL SPECTRUM

	Average Present Rating	Average Future Rating	Difference: Future vs. Present
Operational Spectrum			
Completely liberal	6.62	7.88	+1.26
Predominantly liberal	6.95	7.94	+ .99
Middle of the road	6.90	7.81	+ .91
Predominantly conservative	7.28	8.11	+ .83
Completely conservative	7.70	8.11	+ .41

The important point is that liberals tend not only to be disadvantaged, or less advantaged, than conservatives in an objective economic sense, but they are subjectively aware of being less advantaged in terms of the total spectrum of values by which they judge their lives. They are more aware of unrequited aspirations and unfulfilled needs than the con-

* Average ratings for these and other subgroups of the population are given in Table 7 in Appendix F, pp. 229 f.

servatives, and are thus more favorably disposed toward Governmental policies and programs which might help correct these deficiencies.

Similarly, despite the fact that operational liberals rated themselves lower in the present than did conservatives, the spread between their present and future ratings was greater, as Table VII-5 shows. They expected to make more gains for themselves in the next five years than did conservatives. This greater optimism of the liberals is also evident in the percentages of people whose ladder rating for the future was higher than their rating for the present:

Completely liberal	54%
Predominantly liberal	51
Middle of the road	51
Predominantly conservative	45
Completely conservative	34

The range of expectations from present to future was significantly greater among operational liberals than among conservatives, reflecting the feeling of liberals that the sociopolitical system of the United States, with its "welfare state" overtones, is favorable to their personal progress. Conservatives, on the other hand, caught in their narrower spectrum of expectations, apparently feel the system is not conducive to rapid or pronounced advances on their part but to some extent represents a threat. Partial confirmation of this will be seen when ladder ratings for the country are discussed.

National Aspirations and Fears

The wishes and hopes for the country mentioned by our sample are listed in Table VII-6; the worries and fears in Table VII-7. Again, in both cases items mentioned with a frequency of less than 5 per cent have been omitted. It would

appear that the values Americans apply at the national level
are basically similar to those applied at the personal level,
except that international concerns, predominantly the hope
for peace and the fear of war, are even more prevalent. In
all, 70 per cent of the respondents on their own initiative
described peace as a national hope or war as a national fear,
or both. Additional items brought the total of those naming
one or more international subjects to 76 per cent of the
interviewees. Furthermore, 18 per cent brought up subjects
related to the national status or independence of the United
States, all of which have international implications. Clearly,
the great majority of Americans are highly preoccupied with
at least the elementary aspects of world problems, particularly as they bear on peace, war, and survival.

TABLE VII-6
NATIONAL ASPIRATIONS
(Specified by 5% or more of sample)

Peace	51%
Improved or decent standard of living, greater national prosperity	28
Employment—jobs for everyone	15
Education—more and/or better schools	11
Settlement of racial or integration problems	10
Public morality	10
National unity and political stability	9
The Presidential election	7
Maintenance of status quo	7
Social justice—greater equality for the good of all in the treatment, benefits and opportunities afforded all elements of the population	6
Better world—more international understanding and cooperation	6
Economic stability, no inflation	5
Elimination of discrimination and prejudice based on race, color, etc.	5

TABLE VII-7
NATIONAL FEARS
(Specified by 5% or more of sample)

War	50%
Communism	22
Economic instability, inflation, depression	13
Racial matters	9
National disunity and political instability	8
Socialism or big government—government too powerful or too centralized, too much government interference	8
Threat or aggression by Russia, Communist China, or other communist power	7
Unemployment	6
Lack of public morality	6
No democracy or representative government, totalitarianism	5
Lack of law and order	5
Presidential election	5

The fairly frequent mention of political unity and disunity was no doubt stimulated by the racial riots which occurred during the summer preceding the interviewing. When items such as racial relations, integration, elimination of racial discrimination and the like are added to the picture, it turns out that problems of civil liberty were major preoccupations for at least a third of the sample.

Since our interviewing was conducted during the 1964 Presidential campaign, which, in theory at least, might have been considered crucial in one way or another to the future of America, it is perhaps surprising that the Presidential election was specified by only 7 per cent as one of their national hopes, and by only 5 per cent as one of their national fears. An additional fact is that, among personal wishes and hopes, mention of the election was confined to less than one per cent of the sample, and among personal worries and fears to 2 per cent. As one of those interviewed (an automobile repairman in Michigan) put it: "I suppose I *should* worry about who's going to be President—but I don't."

On the domestic front, the leading items among national aspirations and fears were economic matters such as standard of living and employment, and political items such as communism, socialism, or big government. The frequency with which these subjects occurred differed markedly between operational liberals and conservatives. Liberals put much greater stress on standard of living and employment than conservatives did, while, as would be anticipated, conservatives were more preoccupied with communism, socialism, and big government. Table VII-8 shows the percentages of people who mentioned such subjects either as an aspiration, as a fear, or both. The same tendencies were apparent in answers to the question about Government power. In brief,

TABLE VII-8

SELECTED NATIONAL HOPES AND FEARS OF LIBERALS AND
CONSERVATIVES

	Standard of Living	Employment-Unemployment	Communism	Socialism-Big Government
Operational Spectrum				
Completely liberal	34%	22%	18%	2%
Predominantly liberal	30	19	23	5
Middle of the road	27	17	28	9
Predominantly conservative	25	13	34	24
Completely conservative	18	11	45	29

we see again that operational liberals favor Government action to accomplish the social objectives they believe necessary while operational conservatives are more preoccupied with traditional political ideology at both the personal and national levels.

National Ladder Ratings

When the sample population was asked to rate the United States on the ladder at three points in time—the present, five years in the past, and ten years in the future—the average overall ratings were:

Past	6.12
Present	6.50
Future	7.68

The increase from past to present showed people had a considerable sense of national progress over the preceding five years, while the substantial increment from present to future indicated an underlying sense of optimism about the country's future. The evaluations of many seemed to be summed up by these comments:

Actually, the U.S. has just about everything already. (The wife of the manager of a clothing store in Texas.)

The best thing for the U.S. is to remain as much like it is now as possible. (A Texas importer.)

Things are getting better all the time: more jobs, more tolerance and more money. They're improving all the time. (An office receptionist in California.)

However, this basic picture varied significantly by population groups. Differences in ratings for the present revealed the differing evaluations of the then-current state of the nation.* Higher than average ratings were given by people

* The detailed figures are given in Table 8 in Appendix F, pp. 231 ff.

living in larger cities, by workers, by those with only a grade
school education, and especially by Negroes. The nation was
rated lower than average by people living in cities and towns
under 50,000 population and in rural areas, by professional
and business groups, closely followed by farmers, and by
those with a college education. A special word needs to be
said about the figures according to family income. While the
rating for the present among those in the $3,000–$4,999
bracket was significantly higher than among those with incomes of $5,000 or over, the lowest rating of all was among
families with yearly incomes of less than $3,000.

Another tendency was that people who rated the country
higher than average in the present sensed the greatest national progress from past to present.* This sense of progress
was particularly marked among those with only a grade
school education, blue-collar workers, people living in large
metropolitan centers, and especially Negro Americans. The
spread between past and present ratings among the Negroes
was the greatest among any group in the sample. This keen
sense of national progress in the fall of 1964 was in marked
contrast to results obtained in a similar survey conducted in
1959, when Negroes felt the country had made no progress
at all over the preceding five years.[13] On the other hand, the
college-educated and those in the top income bracket ($10,-
000 and over) had little or no sense of national progress.
And people living in the Southern states that went for
Goldwater in 1964 and those living in rural areas in general,
particularly the farmers, thought the nation had actually
retrogressed.

These configurations foreshadow the marked differences
between liberals and conservatives, both in present ratings

* Again, the figures are given in Table 8 in Appendix F, pp. 231 ff.,
in the column entitled "Difference: Present *vs.* Past."

and in a sense of progress, evident in Table VII-9. Liberals, who rated the past lower and the present higher than conservatives, showed a much more decided sense of progress from past to present than conservatives did. Conservatives, on the other hand, felt the country had drifted backward

TABLE VII-9

NATIONAL LADDER RATINGS FOR PAST AND PRESENT BY
OPERATIONAL SPECTRUM

	Average Past Rating	Average Present Rating	Difference: Present *vs.* Past
Operational Spectrum			
Completely liberal	5.87	6.96	+1.09
Predominantly liberal	6.13	6.62	+ .49
Middle of the road	6.32	6.18	− .14
Predominantly conservative	6.55	5.86	− .69
Completely conservative	6.31	5.12	−1.19

during the preceding five years. The same tendencies were evident no matter how liberalism and conservatism were measured, whether on the Ideological Spectrum, the question regarding Government power, or the question asking respondents to identify themselves on a scale ranging from very liberal to very conservative.* Objectively, all our respondents were looking at the same two national situations —one in 1959, one in 1964—which have been charted on a variety of economic and other objective indices. Yet the way people perceived the state of the nation at these two points in time was vitally affected by their basic political orientations.

* The figures are given in Table 8 in Appendix F, pp. 231 ff.

Optimism and Pessimism

Liberals also felt much more optimistic about the future, as can be seen in Table VII-10 in the "Difference: Future *vs.*

TABLE VII-10

NATIONAL LADDER RATINGS FOR PRESENT AND FUTURE BY
OPERATIONAL SPECTRUM

	Average Present Rating	Average Future Rating	Difference: Future *vs.* Present
Operational Spectrum			
Completely liberal	6.96	8.31	+1.35
Predominantly liberal	6.62	7.85	+1.23
Middle of the road	6.18	7.12	+ .94
Predominantly conservative	5.86	6.67	+ .81
Completely conservative	5.12	5.54	+ .42

Present" column. The percentages of those who rated the present higher than the past and the future higher than the present reveal the same picture of the liberals' greater sense of progress and optimism. For the sake of brevity, Table VII-11 gives results only in terms of the Operational Spectrum, where the differences are most marked. But on the basis of our other measurements of liberalism and conservatism, the generalization still holds that a vastly higher proportion of liberals than of conservatives had a sense of national progress and were optimistic about the future of the United States.

These differences between liberals and conservatives in their perceptions of the trend of their own lives and the life of the nation derived from their different assumptions and values. Liberals, of course, saw the resumption of the New Deal-Fair Deal tradition under President Kennedy and **its**

TABLE VII-11

NATIONAL LADDER RATINGS—PROGRESS AND OPTIMISM BY
OPERATIONAL SPECTRUM

	Per cent Rating	
	Present Higher than Past	Future Higher than Present
Operational Spectrum		
Completely liberal	55%	61%
Predominantly liberal	45	56
Middle of the road	31	49
Predominantly conservative	18	43
Completely conservative	7	34

further implementation in the Great Society program as progress, which engendered hope; conservatives saw the same set of conditions as regression, which dampened optimism at both the personal and national levels. The figures not only show what one would expect but chart the gulf separating these two groups of Americans.

Internationalists vs. Isolationists

The state of the nation must of course be judged not only according to the domestic scene but on the basis of the international situation as well. In this respect, graduated differences appeared in evaluations of people in the various categories of our system of International Patterns. As Table VII-12 shows, the complete internationalists, in line with the current thrust of American foreign policy, rated the nation much higher in the present than did the isolationists, had a greater sense of national progress from past to present, and were more optimistic about the future. The isolationists actually thought the national situation was worse in the present than it had been five years before.

TABLE VII-12

NATIONAL LADDER RATINGS BY INTERNATIONAL PATTERNS

	Average Past Rating	Average Present Rating	Average Future Rating
International Patterns			
Compl. Internationalist	6.10	6.72	7.98
Pred. Internationalist	6.23	6.53	7.81
Mixed	6.10	6.35	7.41
Compl. or Pred. Isol.	5.93	5.86	6.17

	Difference: Present *vs.* Past	Difference: Future *vs.* Present
International Patterns		
Compl. Internationalist	+.62	+1.26
Pred. Internationalist	+.30	+1.28
Mixed	+.25	+1.06
Compl. or Pred. Isol.	−.07	+ .31

When the dimensions of liberalism, conservatism, and internationalism are combined, it is apparent that people who were both liberal and international-minded were those most likely to rate the country highest in the present, to have a sense of national progress, and to be optimistic about the nation's future. At the other end is the little band of isolationist conservatives, out of tune and out of sympathy with current tendencies on both the domestic and international scenes.

VIII

Syndromes and Prejudices

A syndrome is defined in medicine as "a group of signs and symptoms that occur together and characterize a disease." The term is used in the title of this chapter—without any pathological overtones intended—to refer to certain outlooks and attitudes which seem to hang together and are symptomatic of different patterns of thought among liberals and conservatives.

Ideas about Social Dynamics

In accounting for a person's success or failure in life, liberals and conservatives tend to stress different factors. They have divergent views about what might be called the social dynamics that make for success in our culture. Two questions used in our survey tapped these ideas:

QUESTION: Thinking of people now living who are *successful* in life, which three things among those listed on this card do you feel have been chiefly responsible for their success?

QUESTION: Turning to people now living who are *unsuccessful* in life, which three things among those listed on this card do you feel are chiefly responsible for holding them back?

The items listed on the cards and the percentage of people who chose each item, both in the total population and according to their placement on the Operational Spectrum, are given in Tables VIII-1 and VIII-2.

TABLE VIII-1

REASONS FOR SUCCESS BY OPERATIONAL SPECTRUM

	Total Sample	Lib- erals	Middle- Roaders	Conserv- atives
Good education and training	71%	75%	68%	59%
Initiative and effort, hard work	66	61	69	75
Character, will power	59	58	60	70
Born with native intelligence and ability	35	32	39	46
Born into well-to-do family, which gave them better opportunities	23	24	23	13
Good luck, getting the breaks	18	19	16	14
Knew the right people, had "pull"	13	14	10	9
Ruthlessness, clawing their way to the top	5	4	8	8

In accounting for success, liberals put primary stress on education and training, while conservatives emphasized initiative, effort, and hard work, along with character and will power. Similarly, in choosing factors that contribute to failure, liberals gave much greater attention to lack of education and training than to any other item. Conservatives, however, put equal stress on laziness, lack of character, and

TABLE VIII-2
REASONS FOR FAILURE BY OPERATIONAL SPECTRUM

	Total Sample	Lib- erals	Middle- Roaders	Conserv- atives
Lack of education and training	76%	80%	73%	65%
Laziness, little or no ambition	57	53	62	67
Lack of character and will power	47	43	51	65
Lack of native intelligence and ability	32	30	33	39
Limited opportunities	25	26	25	22
Unfavorable family background	17	16	19	16
Bad luck, not getting the breaks	16	17	12	11
Race or religion	14	16	12	8
Too considerate of others to stand up for their own self-interests	7	7	7	4

will power. The same picture emerged when the Ideological Spectrum was used.

Thus, in the eyes of liberals, there is something society can do to help an individual succeed: provide him with education and training. For conservatives, on the other hand, success is more likely to be something an individual must achieve by his own will power and hard work, while failure is largely due to his own laziness and lack of character.

These differences in outlook were reflected in answers to a question, originally discussed in Chapter II, having to do with the reasons for individual poverty:

QUESTION: In your opinion, which is generally more often to blame if a person is poor—lack of effort on his part or circumstances beyond his control?

Table VIII-3 gives the results on the basis of the Ideological Spectrum, where differences were even more marked than on the Operational Spectrum. Ideological liberals saw circumstances as the principal cause of poverty, whereas 85 per cent of the complete conservatives blamed the poor for unadulterated lack of effort, or lack of effort coupled with circumstances. In short, conservatives tend to think failure and poverty are rooted in defects in the human being himself, something governments can do little about. Liberals lean more toward the view that failure and poverty spring primarily from circumstances which governments can ameliorate. Liberals have, it seems, more confidence in human perfectibility under conditions conducive to self-development.

TABLE VIII-3

CAUSES OF POVERTY BY IDEOLOGICAL SPECTRUM

	Liberal	Middle of Road	Predominantly Conservative	Completely Conservative
Circumstances	46%	28%	25%	13%
Lack of effort	15	35	34	48
Both	37	35	39	37
Don't know	2	2	2	2
	100%	100%	100%	100%

Confidence in the People and in the Government

In fact, it appears from another question in our survey that liberals have more trust in the public generally, and hence more confidence in the democratic process. The question and the results for the sample as a whole were as follows:

QUESTION: In general, how much trust and confidence do you have in the wisdom of the American people when it comes to making political decisions—a very great deal, a good deal, not very much, or none at all?

Great deal or good deal	76%
Not very much or none at all	20
Don't know	4
	100%

This overall pattern varied enormously between people who qualified as liberals or as complete conservatives on the Operational Spectrum. Here are the percentages answering "a very great deal" or "a good deal"—in other words, those who showed considerable confidence in the public:

Complete liberals	81%
Predominant liberals	80
Middle-of-the-roaders	75
Predominant conservatives	72
Complete conservatives	54

Among the complete conservatives, 45 per cent said they either did not have very much confidence in the people or had none at all. Also, as would be expected, conservatives expressed much less confidence in the Government. The question used to probe this was a long one:

QUESTION: Now, turning to another subject, our Federal Government, as you know, is made up of three branches: the Executive branch, headed by the President; the Judicial branch, headed by the United States Supreme Court; and the Legislative branch, made up of the United States Senate and House of Representatives. Here is a picture of a ladder. I'd like you to show me on the ladder how much confidence you have in each of these branches, under present circumstances. The top of the ladder in this case means *the greatest possible confidence;* the bottom, *no confidence at all.* First, how much trust and confidence do you have in the Executive branch, headed by the President?

Secondly, in the Judicial branch, headed by the United States Supreme Court?

And, finally, in the Legislative branch, made up of the Senate and House of Representatives?

It will be recalled that the highest possible score on the ladder is ten and the lowest zero. The results both for the total sample and on the basis of the Operational Spectrum are given in Table VIII-4. The "Average" column, calculated by averaging the ratings of the three branches, shows that liberals had much more confidence in the Government as a whole than did conservatives.

TABLE VIII-4

CONFIDENCE IN BRANCHES OF GOVERNMENT
BY OPERATIONAL SPECTRUM

	Averages for Executive	Averages for Legislative	Averages for Judicial	Overall Average
National Averages	7.43	7.23	6.89	7.18
Operational Spectrum				
Completely liberal	8.40	7.54	7.91	7.95
Predominantly liberal	7.65	7.40	6.97	7.34
Middle of the road	7.02	7.13	6.44	6.86
Predominantly conservative	5.79	6.75	5.50	6.01
Completely conservative	4.07	6.01	3.72	4.60

Within this general pattern, while liberals gave the highest rating to the Executive branch, the conservatives' highest rating by far went to the Legislative branch, which they apparently considered something of a bulwark against the liberalism of the other two branches. As a retired worker in Mississippi put it: "Let the Senate and House have more power—and take it away from the Federal courts."

Communism and Socialism

Conservatives, of course, agreed with the statement that "there is a definite trend toward socialism in this country" much more than did liberals. On the basis of the Ideological Spectrum—where the differences were more marked than on the Operational Spectrum since the matter has such ideological overtones—the conservatives tended to agree and the liberals to disagree with this related statement: "There is too much Communist and left-wing influence in our Government these days." Typical comments on the part of those who agreed were as follows:

I am contented right now—except that I'd like to get some of the pinks and reds out of our Government. (A sheet metal worker in New York City.)

I fear that persons in key positions in the Government are aiding Communism through deceptive means. (A teacher in Georgia.)

There are so many Communists in our Government. I hope that they will not be allowed to take over. (An unemployed widow in Florida.)

Another question in our survey demonstrated how widespread the fear of Communists is among Americans:

QUESTION: How much danger do you think the Communists right here in America are to this country at the present time?

A very great deal	28%
A good deal	34
Not very much	29
None at all	3
Don't know	6
	100%

Some seemed to see a Communist under every bed:

I also have a fear of the Communists. They seem to be everywhere. (A butcher in Indiana.)

I don't understand a lot about the Communists, but I sure fear them. (A retired woman living in Tennessee.)

You hear that the Communists are already here and more are coming. (A farmer's wife in North Carolina.)

If the "great deal" and "good deal" replies to this question are combined, there appears a marked gradation on the Ideological Spectrum, with three-fourths of the complete conservatives feeling that Communists present at least a good deal of danger:

	Great Deal
Ideological Spectrum	*or Good Deal*
Completely or predominantly liberal	46%
Middle of the road	56
Predominantly conservative	68
Completely conservative	76

Thus, some of the symptoms connected with the conservative syndrome consist of fear of socialism, of left-wing influence, and of Communists.

Negroes and Civil Rights

The following opinion surveys highlight the change in attitudes toward integration and civil rights that has occurred in this country during the past quarter of a century. In June of 1942, the National Opinion Research Center asked these questions of a national cross section of Americans, including Negroes, of course:

QUESTION: Generally speaking, do you think there should be separate sections for Negroes in street cars and buses?

Yes	51%
No	44
Don't know	5
	100%

QUESTION: Do you think there should be separate restaurants for Negroes and white people?

Yes	69%
No	27
Don't know	4
	100%

QUESTION: Do you think there should be separate sections in towns and cities for Negroes to live in?

Yes	84%
No	14
Don't know	2
	100%

The Gallup Poll found during the early stages of World War II that a majority of the public (Negroes not excluded) thought that "the average Negro makes just as good a soldier as the average white man" (June 20, 1942). But at the same time, one-half were opposed to integration of the armed forces:

QUESTION: Should Negro and white soldiers serve together in all branches of the armed forces? (June 9, 1942.)

Yes	41%
No	51
No opinion	8
	100%

Twenty-two years later, the results of our own survey of a national cross section show that six out of ten Americans approved the sweeping civil rights law passed by Congress and signed by the President in the summer of 1964, shortly before our interviewing began. Opinion about this measure varied dramatically on the basis of our Operational Spectrum. Here are the percentages of those who approved:

Completely liberal	74%
Predominantly liberal	62
Middle of the road	53
Predominantly conservative	37
Completely conservative	24

These results indicated what liberals would undoubtedly charge is anti-Negro bias on the part of conservatives. Additional data from our survey show, however, that liberals themselves were by no means entirely free of bias, although less prejudiced than conservatives. For example, at a time when J. Edgar Hoover himself was affirming that, as of then, the civil rights movement had not been infiltrated by the Communists, we tested the following statement:

STATEMENT: Most of the organizations pushing for civil rights have been infiltrated by the Communists and are now dominated by Communist trouble-makers.

The "agree" figures on the basis of the Operational Spectrum were as follows:

Completely liberal	39%
Predominantly liberal	49
Middle of the road	53
Predominantly conservative	60
Completely conservative	71

A related question and results from the total sample follow:

QUESTION: In your opinion, are the Negroes who have been participating in the recent rioting and violence chiefly just bad characters without respect for law and order, or are they victims of despair and lack of opportunity?

Bad characters	37%
Victims of despair	25
Both or neither	32
Don't know	6
	100%

Only one operational conservative in ten answered "victims of despair." But even among the complete liberals on the Operational Spectrum and though Negroes were included in the sample, slightly more saw the rioters as just plain trouble-makers than saw them as victims of despair and lack of opportunity.

There was another question concerning the pace of integration:

QUESTION: On the whole, do you think that racial integration of Negroes in this country is going ahead too fast or not fast enough?

Too fast	56%
About right	18
Not fast enough	20
No opinion	6
	100%

While a large majority of conservatives felt integration was going ahead too rapidly, a plurality of the complete liberals on the Operational Spectrum also agreed, as Table VIII-5 shows.

Finally, people (including Negroes) were asked whether they would like to see Negroes "have *more* influence in government and political matters than they have now, or

TABLE VIII-5

PACE OF INTEGRATION BY OPERATIONAL SPECTRUM

	Too Fast	About Right	Not Fast Enough	No Opin-ion	Total
Completely liberal	44%	25%	25%	6%	100%
Predominantly liberal	61	17	20	2	100
Middle of the road	63	16	15	6	100
Predominantly conservative	75	17	5	3	100
Completely conservative	82	9	4	5	100

less influence than they have now?" The overall results were as follows:

More influence	30%
Less influence	31
Present influence about right	28
No opinion	11
	100%

From the point of view of practical politics, Negro influence was still minimal at the time of our survey in the fall of 1964. Yet one-fifth of the complete liberals and one-third of the predominantly liberal answered "less influence." The figures are given in Table VIII-6. It should be added that data based on the Ideological Spectrum showed that, while the proportion of ideological liberals who were prejudiced was less than that of operational liberals, it was still significant.

Sharp differences in outlook among American whites regarding the Negro problem were revealed by some of the comments of those interviewed. First, here are illustrations of anti-Negro sentiment:

TABLE VIII-6

INFLUENCE OF NEGROES BY OPERATIONAL SPECTRUM

	Comp. Lib.	Pred. Lib.	Middle of Road	Pred. Cons.	Compl. Cons.
Negroes should have more influence	37%	34%	23%	21%	18%
Should have less influence	21	35	35	45	60
Present influence about right	30	27	28	25	14
No opinion	12	4	14	9	8
	100%	100%	100%	100%	100%

I am afraid that the colored people will take over. Giving them equal rights is all wrong. We will be discriminated against by the colored people. They'll be able to push us around, take our jobs. They'll take over the country. (A painting contractor in Arizona.)

Well, I just believe that the niggers and the whites are going to have war. (A North Carolina worker.)

After stating that his hope was for peace on earth, "where people can get along and not claw back and forth at one another," one respondent went on to mention this additional aspiration:

That Washington would leave the Negro alone. The Southern Negro is happy with the way things were. He doesn't want to live with the whites. Suppose there was a group of whites outside in front of my house and a Negro joined them. That wouldn't look right, would it? (A vending machine serviceman in Wisconsin.)

My hope is to stop this terrible mixing of white and colored, especially in the schools—the white girls having colored babies. (A housewife in West Virginia.)

The way the Negroes are making trouble, they pretty soon will get on top of the whites. We may even have a Negro President. (A retired man living in Michigan.)

I would like the niggers to go back to being niggers and the whites to being whites. They would still have their rights. (A housewife in Louisiana.)

I would like to be able to choose my own friends and neighbors without the Government shoving the Negroes down my throat. . . . I don't have anything in particular against Negroes. (A bus driver in Virginia.)

They should ship all the Negroes back to Africa. (The wife of an Air Force sergeant stationed in Kansas.)

The Communists is coming in. They are working through the colored people in all this here trouble. (A millworker in North Carolina.)

On the other hand, those whites favoring integration and equal rights said things such as these:

I hope the Negroes will be able to obtain an educational level that will gain them acceptance and equal opportunities with the white people, and that this can be reached in a nonviolent way. (A financial analyst in Michigan.)

It's not a man's fault that his skin is black. (A worker in Wisconsin.)

I'd like to see all people happy and contented, all racial differences settled. I'd like to see the poor and unfortunate people helped to better themselves. I'd like to see all Negroes and other minorities treated as equals and not pushed down. (The wife of an insurance salesman living in Massachusetts.)

This integration thing is important. Negroes have a right to live. White trash is worse. If we're to set an example, they're human, just like everyone else. We have to give them their rights. (The wife of a filling station attendant in California.)

The Negroes are Americans and should be treated as such. But they also should not ask more than the white people and should stand on their own two feet. (A male high school teacher in Oregon.)

As for the Negroes themselves, some of their remarks had a good deal of poignancy:

I would like freedom. (The Negro wife of a construction worker in Milwaukee.)

I would like to be treated as a human being. I would like to raise my unborn children in a world without hate or fear and free from prejudice. (The Negro wife of a merchant seaman living in New Orleans.)

Will *my* children be able to go to college? They have a dark skin. (A Negro child counsellor employed by the State of Washington.)

My hope is to see a Negro treated equal—hired for what he is qualified for—treated as a first-class citizen. (A New Orleans Negro worker.)

Some of us can't even join a union. Just a better chance to get good jobs, that's all. (A Negro worker in Detroit.)

I want my children to have a good education, to be good citizens and to qualify for jobs that will pay enough to support their families. I want them to grow up in peace and prove that color has nothing to do with ability to be a good neighbor and citizen. (The Negro wife of a truck driver in Utah.)

I don't expect the Government to do everything. I want them to be fair, but my people have to work to help themselves when they are given an equal opportunity. (A retired Negro living in Detroit.)

Catholics and Jews

Differences between liberals and conservatives also arose in answers to questions as to whether Roman Catholics and Jews should have more influence or less in governmental and political matters. The answers from the sample as a whole, including members of both faiths, came out thus with respect to Catholics:

Catholics should have more influence	9%
Should have less influence	24
Present influence about right	47
No opinion	20
	100%

The corresponding figures with regard to Jews were as follows:

Jews should have more influence	8%
Should have less influence	20
Present influence about right	47
No opinion	25
	100%

Considering the extent of anti-Catholic and anti-Jewish prejudice which has existed in this country in the past, the "less influence" figures, indicating prejudice, do not appear high in either case. However, on the Operational Spectrum, the "less influence" percentages were graduated as follows:

	Catholics	Jews
Completely liberal	18%	16%
Predominantly liberal	26	21
Middle of the road	28	24
Predominantly conservative	32	24
Completely conservative	41	27

Again, it was the conservatives who displayed the most bias, particularly against Catholics, but the liberals were not entirely free of it either, although both groups were less prejudiced against Catholics and Jews than against Negroes.

Labor Unions

Our results revealed that a majority in the United States was in favor of increased controls over labor unions. Here are the reactions to one of the statements put to the sample population:

STATEMENT: Labor unions should be subject to more governmental controls and regulations.

Agree	52%
Disagree	30
No opinion	18
	100%

Significantly, four out of ten who belonged to a union themselves or whose spouse did agreed with this statement. On this question of controls, there was relatively little difference between complete liberals on our Operational Spectrum (48 per cent of whom agreed) and complete conservatives (53 per cent of whom agreed).

An additional question also demonstrated that a majority of the American public was somewhat anti-union at this stage. Our respondents were asked whether unions should have more or less influence on government and political matters, with these results:

Unions should have more influence	17%
Should have less influence	49
Present influence about right	20
No opinion	14
	100%

Some of the comments were indicative of strong anti-union feeling:

> I would like to see the power of labor unions curbed severely. Basically I believe in unions, but they have too much power now. (An employee in an atomic energy plant in Washington State.)

> I don't think we need worry about anything but the unions. They operate on a basis where the Government can't touch them. They have too much control over the working man. They can tell him what to do and, if he doesn't do it, he's out of a job. Our unions have too much power. (A retired Oregonian.)

> Something will have to be done about the labor unions or they will take over, and that would be the nearest thing to Communism. (The wife of a plumber in Ohio.)

> I'd like to see laws protecting industry as well as labor. I don't think we'll ever destroy labor unions, as such. I don't think it would be good if we did. But, I think we should take the teeth out of the labor unions to control the nation. I don't think, for example, that Hoffa's Teamsters Union should be able to tie up our nation. And I don't think that sort of thing can continue under a free enterprise system in a free America. (An automobile man and member of the John Birch Society in California.)

In answering our question dealing with influence rather than controls, operational liberals turned out to be very much less anti-union than conservatives. As shown in Table VIII-7, one-third of the complete liberals felt unions should have less influence, compared with nine out of ten of the complete conservatives.

TABLE VIII-7
INFLUENCE OF LABOR UNIONS BY OPERATIONAL SPECTRUM

	Compl. Lib.	Pred. Lib.	Middle of Road	Pred. Cons.	Compl. Cons.
Unions should have more influence	23%	17%	18%	11%	1%
Should have less influence	33	50	64	69	92
Present influence about right	26	24	12	12	2
No opinion	18	9	6	8	5
	100%	100%	100%	100%	100%

Big Business

While a majority of the public was in favor of additional controls on labor unions, most people apparently did not feel it was necessary to break up huge corporations:

QUESTION: During the past ten years there have been a number of corporations that have done more than a *billion* dollars' worth of business each year. Which of these four statements [listed on a card] comes closest to describing your own feeling about a corporation that does this much business?

1. It is dangerous for the welfare of the country for any companies to be this big and they should be broken up into smaller companies.   13%

2. While it may be necessary to have some very large companies, we should watch their activities very closely and discourage their growth as much as possible.   17

3. There may be some reasons against having such

large corporations, but on the whole they do
more good than harm to the country.   31%

4. It is foolish to worry about a company just because it is big; large companies have made
America the kind of country it is today.   29

Don't know   10
                                                            ─────
                                                            100%

Answers unfavorable to big business (the first and second)
total only 30 per cent, compared to a total of 60 per cent who
chose the favorable alternatives (the third and fourth).
There were no differences of any real significance on this
question between liberals and conservatives.

People were also asked whether "large business corporations" should have more or less influence on government
and political matters. The figures for the sample as a whole
were weighted toward the anti-big-business side:

Large corporations should have
     more influence   12%
Should have less influence   43
Present influence about right   25
No opinion   20
                                                            ─────
                                                            100%

A surprise came when the answers to this question were
sorted out by liberals and conservatives on the Operational
Spectrum: the conservatives were more opposed to big
business than the liberals. Here are the "less influence"
figures on the basis of the Operational Spectrum:

Completely liberal   38%
Predominantly liberal   44
Middle of the road   54
Predominantly conservative   51
Completely conservative   50

The most plausible interpretation of this result would seem to be that conservatives, as a matter of principle, are more distrustful than liberals of any major element in our society having too much power and influence—whether it be Government, labor unions, or big business. They view excessive power or influence as a threat to the individual. Liberals, on the other hand, have become adjusted, or resigned, to the facts of life in twentieth century America—where big government, big labor, and big business all enjoy immense powers.

IX

Political Identifications

Proportion of Republicans, Democrats, and Independents

At the time of the 1964 elections, our study, as well as the then-current Gallup surveys, showed that when samples of the national adult population were asked, "In politics as of today, do you consider yourself a Republican, Democrat, or Independent?" about one-half identified themselves as Democrats, about one-fourth as Republicans, and about one-fourth as Independents, with only very small percentages naming other parties or saying they didn't know. Since that time, in the wake of the 1966 elections, the proportion of Democrats has dropped by four percentage points and the percentage of Republicans has risen by two, so that the figures at the present writing are: Democrats 44 per cent; Republicans 29 per cent; Independents 27 per cent (Gallup: December 21, 1966). Despite this shift, it is obvious that Democrats still greatly outnumber Republicans, while one out of every four respondents refuses to associate himself with either party.

As would be expected, Independents tend much more than Democrats or Republicans to be "swing voters." They also show a proclivity toward ticket-splitting. For example, a majority of Independents voted Democratic in the 1958 Congressional elections, while in the succeeding elections in 1962, a majority opted for the Republican side (Gallup: July 31, 1966). Similarly, in 1964, 56 per cent of the Independents cast their votes for President Johnson, but in 1966 exactly the same percentage indicated they were going to vote for Republican congressmen (Gallup: November 2, 1966). In some elections, as many as 75 per cent of the Independents split their tickets (Gallup: July 31, 1966).

The most significant aspect of these figures is not that one-fourth of the public consider themselves "Independents," but that three-fourths identify themselves psychologically with one or the other of the two major parties—an identification which seems to have real meaning for them. At the practical level of political behavior, many split their tickets, or vote—occasionally or even frequently—for candidates of the opposition party. (Gallup Poll figures show, for example, that as many as 23 per cent of the Democrats indicated an intention to vote for Republican Eisenhower in 1952 and as many as 20 per cent of the Republicans for Johnson in 1964.) Nevertheless, party allegiances tend to remain relatively stable and enduring: if a person once identifies himself in his own mind as a Democrat or a Republican, he is more likely than not to continue doing so throughout his political life,[14] although there are of course many individual exceptions.

Party allegiances tend to be transmitted from one generation to the next to a considerable extent.[15] In our study, for example, 56 per cent of those whose father or mother habitually voted Republican also classified themselves as Republicans; and 66 per cent of those whose father or mother voted Democratic labelled themselves Democrats. Democratic-voting parents exceeded Republican-voting parents by about two to one; and at the same time more offspring of Democrats than of Republicans adopted their parents' allegiances—a not-too-promising prospect for the Republican Party.

Party Differences

One sometimes hears it said that there is little difference between our two major parties. Compared with the range of disagreement existing in countries where the political spectrum runs from parties of the extreme right to parties of the extreme left, this is no doubt correct. But it is true only up to a point. The differences that do exist between Republicans and Democrats have become obscured by the fact that, until the 1964 election when the Republican candidate did, indeed, offer "a choice, not an echo," in recent times the Presidential candidates of both parties have tended to be "moderates," both seeking votes from middle-of-the-road voters and Independents. Thus, the distinctions between what they advocated have appeared to be more of emphasis than of substance. If we examine the attitudes of people who habitually identify themselves with each of the two parties, however, differences do exist, some slight, others marked.

In Chapter VI on "International Outlooks," for example, we saw that Republicans by and large tended to be less internationalist than Democrats. Correspondingly, a much larger proportion of Republicans were in favor of reducing or terminating foreign aid. Republicans also leaned a great deal more toward the "hawk" side, favoring stronger measures against Cuba and escalation of the war in Vietnam. More of them were also of the opinion that the United States should take a firmer stand against Russia. A plurality of Republicans, but not of Democrats, were opposed to the United States' establishing diplomatic relations with Communist China. The proportion agreeing that the United States should maintain its dominant position in the world, even going to the brink of war if necessary, was higher among Republicans than among Democrats. In all respects, Republicans were inclined to be less internationalist and more nationalist than Democrats and to choose oftener the "hard line."

Liberalism and Conservatism

The greatest difference between rank-and-file Republicans and Democrats, however, is in their domestic outlook, as reflected in our measurements of liberalism and conservatism. Table IX-1 gives the results on the basis of the Operational Spectrum. Only half as many Republicans as Democrats qualified as operational liberals, the Independents being almost exactly in between. Similarly, almost half of the Republicans felt the Government had too much power, while three-fourths of the Democrats were of the opinion that it has about the right amount of power or should use its powers even more vigorously. Again, the Independents took a mid-way position on this question. Far more Democrats than Republicans favored the Government using its power and resources to accomplish social objectives, with Independents leaning toward the same view but by no means so strongly.

TABLE IX-1

OPERATIONAL SPECTRUM BY PARTY

	Republicans		Independents		Democrats	
Operational Spectrum						
Completely liberal	21%	} 41%	35%	} 59%	58%	} 79%
Predominantly liberal	20		24		21	
Middle of the road	30	} 30	24	} 24	16	} 16
Predominantly conservative	14	} 29	10	} 17	3	} 5
Completely conservative	15		7		2	
	100%		100%		100%	

As Table IX-2 shows, differences were equally marked on the Ideological Spectrum. Thus, a majority of Republicans are middle of the road or conservative at the operational level of Government programs while a very large majority of Democrats are liberal. At the ideological level, a huge majority of Republicans are conservative while two-thirds of the Democrats are either middle of the road or liberal.

TABLE IX-2

IDEOLOGICAL SPECTRUM BY PARTY

	Republicans	Independents	Democrats
Ideological Spectrum			
Completely or predominantly liberal	6%	16%	22%
Middle of the road	22	29	42
Predominantly conservative	23 }72%	20 }55%	17 }36%
Completely conservative	49	35	19
	100%	100%	100%

It is evident that at the rank-and-file level there are fundamental differences in outlook and orientation between Democrats and Republicans. The Independents were a special case: a majority of them were operational liberals, but, at the same time, a majority were also ideological conservatives. This may help explain the ambivalence of the Independents' political behavior: they are pulled in different directions by conflicting orientations which increases their tendency toward vote-switching and ticket-splitting.

Parental Influence

We have noted that there is a certain amount of transference of party allegiance from one generation to the next.

Parental influence also seems to have a bearing on the liberal or conservative outlook of their offspring. To trace this more precisely, respondents were asked to place their father as well as themselves on the liberal-conservative scale discussed in Chapter IV. The relation between self-identification and father-identification is given in Table IX-3. The interesting fact here is that, for the most part, the offspring tend to be one step more conservative than their fathers except that the offspring of "very conservative" parents shift heavily over to the liberal side. Apparently the child rebels against what he considers the extreme conservatism of his father.

TABLE IX-3

FATHER AS LIBERAL OR CONSERVATIVE BY OFFSPRING'S IDENTIFICATION

	Father Identified As				
	Very Lib.	Mod. Lib.	Middle of Road	Mod. Cons.	Very Cons.
Offspring Is					
Very liberal	6%	2%	2%	2%	45%
Moderately liberal	58	14	15	12	21
Middle of road	22	69	25	24	19
Moderately conservative	13	13	53	35	10
Very conservative	1	2	5	27	5
	100%	100%	100%	100%	100%

Both the influence of the father on the liberal-conservative outlook at the practical level and the rebellion against the very conservative parent showed up on the Operational Spectrum as well, as shown in Table IX-4. A large majority of those whose fathers were "very liberal" proved to be operational liberals. From there, the percentage of liberals tends to drop until one reaches those whose fathers were "very conservative," among whom the "completely liberal" figure on the Operational Spectrum is as high as among those whose fathers were "very liberal."

TABLE IX-4

FATHER As LIBERAL OR CONSERVATIVE BY OFFSPRING'S RATING ON
OPERATIONAL SPECTRUM

	Father Identified As				
	Very Lib.	Mod. Lib.	Middle of Road	Mod. Cons.	Very Cons.
Offspring Qualified on Operational Spectrum As					
Completely liberal	51%⎫	43%⎫	34%⎫	29%⎫	51%⎫
Predominantly liberal	25 ⎬76%	20 ⎬63%	18 ⎬52%	24 ⎬53%	23 ⎬74%
Middle of road	16	25	27	25	19
Predominantly conservative	5 ⎫	7 ⎫	11 ⎫	9 ⎫	3 ⎫
Completely conservative	3 ⎬8	5 ⎬12	10 ⎬21	13 ⎬22	4 ⎬7
	100%	100%	100%	100%	100%

Patterns of Concerns

Republicans, Democrats, and Independents differ in the degree to which they are concerned about the twenty-three problems or issues described in Chapter V on "The Concerns of Americans." It will be recalled that the maximum possible degree of concern under our rating system was indicated by a score of 300; the minimum, by a score of zero. When it came to the international items in the list, the average scores for International Concerns were almost the same among Republicans (232), Democrats (231), and Independents (230). However, as Table IX-5 shows, there were marked differences in the case of domestic items which made up our average score for Operational Concerns (education, Medicare, unemployment, and poverty) and for Ideological Concerns (individual liberties, free enterprise, the trend toward a more powerful Federal Government, and states' rights). Democrats were much more concerned about operational matters than Republicans and Independents, and their average score for Operational Concerns was much higher than their score for Ideological Concerns. On the other hand, Republicans were the least concerned of the three groups about operational items and much more concerned about ideological matters. Independents again were in between. Republicans were also much more concerned about Government spending (236) than Democrats (186), with Independents in the middle (207).

TABLE IX-5

SCORES ON OPERATIONAL AND IDEOLOGICAL CONCERNS BY PARTY

	Republicans	Independents	Democrats
Operational Concerns	198	212	229
Ideological Concerns	213	202	186

With respect to domestic concerns, the Democratic pattern corresponds to that found among liberals in Chapter V, and the Republican pattern to that among conservatives, with the pattern among Independents being a mixture of the two. Democrats are more pragmatically or operationally oriented; Republicans are more ideological-minded; Independents are both ideological and pragmatic.

Differing orientations also appeared in regard to personal aspirations and fears. As did the liberals described in Chapter VII, the Democrats stressed more than Republicans did their personal economic or living conditions, employment and unemployment, and opportunities for their children— all matters the Government can and is doing something about. As did the conservatives, Republicans put greater emphasis than Democrats on political or ideological matters. Republicans also included Communism and big government or socialism among their national worries and fears much more often than did Democrats.

Class Identifications

Marked differences also appeared in the way Republicans, Democrats, and Independents identify their interests with the propertied class, the middle class, or the working class, as seen in Table IX-6. Republicans tended to associate their own interests with those of either the propertied or the middle classes, while the Democrats identified predominantly with the working class. Independents were split down the middle.

TABLE IX-6

CLASS IDENTIFICATION BY PARTY

	Republicans	Independents	Democrats
Identify Interests with			
Propertied class	11% ⎫	5% ⎫	2% ⎫
Middle class	50 ⎬ 61%	41 ⎬ 46%	29 ⎬ 31%
Working class	35 ⎭	46 ⎭	65 ⎭
Don't know	4	8	4
	100%	100%	100%

Both on the score of liberalism-conservatism and of subjective class identifications, it is no wonder that a majority of Americans have an image of the Democratic Party as the party of "labor, the common man, all the people," and of the Republican Party as the party of "the moneyed interests and the privileged few" (Gallup: February 3, 1954). An Iowa painter expressed this notion in highly exaggerated fashion: "The Republicans represent aristocrats and millionaires; the Democrats represent the will of the working class of people." A survey conducted by the Opinion Research Corporation shortly before the 1964 elections confirmed these images. When asked which party is on the workingman's side, 45 per cent named the Democratic Party and only 7 per cent the Republican, the rest replying either "both" or "neither" or saying they had no opinion. At the same time, 37 per cent said the Republican Party favored big business too much, as compared with only 8 per cent who felt this way about the Democratic Party. To show how pervasive this part of the image is, 25 per cent of those identifying themselves as Republicans agreed that their own party favored big business too much. No wonder, then, that when Gallup polled GOP county chairmen across the nation, 59 per cent of them agreed with President Eisenhower that the Republican Party had a "bad image" (January 22, 1965).

As a result, in 1963 at least, when asked "which political party—the Republican or Democratic—do you think best serves the interest of people like yourself?" twice as many Americans named the Democratic Party as named the Republican (Gallup: May 12, 1963). Later (February 28, 1965), Gallup asked this same question of representative samples of persons in families from major occupational groups. The results are given in Table IX-7, where only the percentages for the Republican Party and the Democratic Party are listed; the percentages of those who said there was no difference between the two parties in this respect or who had no opinion are omitted. It will be seen that only the professional and business people think the Republican Party serves the interests of their own group best.

TABLE IX-7
PARTY BEST FOR SELF

	Republican	Democratic
Professional and business people	56%	22%
White collar workers	27	39
Farmers	20	52
Skilled workers	15	59
Unskilled workers	8	62

Demographic Differences

The general outline of the respective strengths and weaknesses of the Republican and Democratic parties among subgroups of the population is well known to all students of politics. Our study showed that while less numerous than the Democrats, the Republicans had a proportionately greater following among those fifty years of age or older, in the professional and business group, among Protestants, among people living in the Midwest, and among those residing in places of under 50,000 population or in rural areas than they did in other population groups.* In only two related groups did those who identified themselves as Republicans outnumber those who identified themselves as Democrats: the college-educated and those with an annual income of $10,000 or more. Democrats, on the other hand, were even more numerous among those with less than a college education, among blue-collar workers, among those with incomes of less than $10,000, among people living in the East and in the South, among those in cities of over 50,000 population, and particularly among Negroes, than they were in other groups.

* See Table 9 in Appendix F, pp. 233 ff.

Except in the South, which at this point remains an anomaly, this pattern obviously corresponds with the differences in the patterns for operational liberals and conservatives reported in Chapter II on "Government Programs and Governmental Power." As Table IX-8 shows, there is a close correspondence, in fact, between the percentages in each group who qualified as "completely liberal" on the Operational Spectrum and the proportion who identified themselves as Democrats. In brief, the larger the proportion of operational liberals in general, and of those "completely liberal" in particular, the higher the percentage in each group who considered themselves Democrats. The converse is of course also true: the lower the proportion of liberals, the higher the percentage of Republicans. The same tendencies appeared on the Ideological Spectrum.

Nor is this any wonder. Despite the presence in Congress of many conservative Democrats, especially Southerners, who frequently have great power as committee chairmen, the image the public has of the Democratic Party is a liberal one, imparted by a series of Democratic Chief Executives operating in the tradition of the New Deal, Fair Deal, New Frontier, and Great Society. It is only natural that those favoring use of Government power and resources to accomplish social objectives should gravitate toward that party. On the other hand, in recent history, the Republican Party's image has been determined primarily by Republicans in Congress, the majority of whom were conservatives who have, initially at least, opposed most major extensions of Federal power as a matter of principle.

Religious Differences

Up to this point, the patterns revealed by the polls are what would be expected and seem to make sense. Quite understandably, the Democratic Party attracts liberals, people

TABLE IX-8

Per cent Complete Liberals on Operational Spectrum
and Per cent Democrats

	Compl. Liberals	Democrats
Education		
Grade school	54%	58%
High school	42	50
College	32	34
Income		
Under $5,000	52	55
$5,000–$9,999	41	50
$10,000 and over	32	34
Occupation		
Professional and business	33	37
White-collar workers	39	45
Farmers	34	44
Blue-collar workers	51	57
Nonlabor	44	51
Race		
White	40	45
Negro	79	87
City Size		
500,000 and over	55	54
50,000–499,999	43	56
2,500–49,999	31	41
Under 2,500 and rural	36	44

who tend to be less advantaged and more preoccupied with
problems and needs which in their eyes can be alleviated by
the kinds of Governmental programs which Democratic administrations have advocated and inaugurated, starting with

Political Identifications

the New Deal. But our figures show a phenomenon which
is difficult to explain in these terms: 63 per cent of the
Roman Catholics and 65 per cent of the Jews identified
themselves as Democrats, compared with only 45 per cent of
the Protestants. Yet our study showed that Jews enjoy a much
higher socioeconomic status than Protestants and that even
Catholics have now more than caught up with Protestants
in this area. It is simply no longer true that Catholics are
less well off and less well educated than Protestants. The
relative status of the three religious groups is of such importance in the social fabric of the United States today that
we give a comparative analysis of their education, income,
and occupations in Table IX-9.

TABLE IX-9

EDUCATION, INCOME, AND OCCUPATION BY RELIGION

	Protestant	Catholic	Jewish
Education			
College	18%	18%	33%
High school	47	55	45
Grade school	35	27	22
	100%	100%	100%
Income			
$10,000 and over	15%	18%	29%
$5,000–$9,999	38	46	55
Under $5,000	47	36	16
	100%	100%	100%
Occupation			
Professional and business	20%	23%	46%
White-collar workers	9	12	25
Farmers	8	3	—
Blue-collar workers	43	51	18
Non-labor	19	10	9
Undesignated	1	1	2
	100%	100%	100%

On the basis of socioeconomic status alone, Catholics should be no more Democratic than Protestants and Jews much less so. Yet the reverse is the case. This study can go only a short way in trying to explain this phenomenon. Fundamentally, Catholics and Jews are much more Democratic than Protestants because, despite their socioeconomic status, they are much more liberal in their orientations. Table IX-10 reveals this in terms of the Operational Spectrum.

TABLE IX-10

OPERATIONAL SPECTRUM BY RELIGION

	Protestant	Catholic	Jewish
Operational Spectrum			
Completely liberal	38% } 60%	55% } 77%	69% } 90%
Predominantly liberal	22	22	21
Middle of the road	22	17	7
Predominantly conservative	9	3	*
Completely conservative	9	3	3
	100%	100%	100%

* Less than one-half of one per cent

The same tendency was evident on the Ideological Spectrum as Table IX-11 shows. The Jews represent the only population subgroup in our study among whom ideological liberals actually constituted a plurality; Negroes were the only group approaching them in this respect. While the idea of Jewish liberalism sounds neither new nor strange, as recently as the fall of 1965 an associate editor of a leading Catholic publication wrote: "Politically, the American Catholic has tended to be conservative, suspicious of central government." [16] Assuming this may once have been the case, we can only say that it is no longer so: 77 per cent of American

TABLE IX-11

IDEOLOGICAL SPECTRUM BY RELIGION

	Protestant	Catholic	Jewish
Ideological Spectrum			
Completely or predominantly liberal	14%	17%	44%
Middle of the road	28	48	39
Predominantly conservative	21 ⎫ 58%	18 ⎫ 35%	10 ⎫ 17%
Completely conservative	37 ⎭	17 ⎭	7 ⎭
	100%	100%	100%

Catholics qualified as liberal on our Operational Spectrum, only 13 per cent thought the Federal Government had too much power, and 38 per cent felt the Government should use its powers even more vigorously.

The data offer only partial evidence for the following speculations about the reasons for Catholic and Jewish liberalism. To start on solid ground, we have found that urban living makes for liberal orientations, and both of these groups are much more highly urbanized than Protestants. Seventy-nine per cent of the Catholics in this country live in cities of over 50,000 population, compared with 46 per cent of the Protestants; and no less than 85 per cent of the Jews reside in metropolitan areas of over 500,000 population.

Secondly, both of these groups are in large part descendants of people who came to America in the more recent waves of immigration. When their ancestors arrived in the United States, they were, indeed, disadvantaged minority groups. It is our belief that, despite their spectacular socioeconomic progress since, the habit of perceiving themselves as members of disadvantaged minority groups still persists to some extent—a habit which encourages a liberal outlook.

More concretely, for a variety of reasons applicable to most recent immigrant groups, a majority of Catholics and Jews early developed the habit of considering themselves Democrats. This was chiefly because the Democratic Party, much more than the Republican, assumed the role of champion of disadvantaged minorities and worked to win their allegiance. Witness, for example, the aid and comfort furnished newly arrived immigrants by Tammany Hall and other Democratic political machines in the big cities, ranging from locating jobs for them to supplying food, coal, clothing, and money in time of need. Later, the equalitarian orientation of the New Deal and subsequent Democratic administrations undoubtedly strengthened this Democratic appeal. It is our guess, in short, that the allegiance to the Democratic Party as an institution, initially created at an early date, had a reinforcing effect in developing and perpetuating liberal outlooks among Catholics and Jews as the Party, beginning especially with Franklin D. Roosevelt, followed the path of increasing liberalism.

Ethnic Groups

A phenomenon roughly similar to that posed by the Democratic leanings of Catholics and Jews is presented by the descendants of those who came to America in the more recent waves of immigration. To analyze this, we classified our white respondents (Negro Americans were excluded as constituting a separate ethnic group) in two categories: (1) those with no grandparents born in the United States (many of them of Italian, East European, or Central European origin), and (2) those with some or all grandparents born in this country. As it turned out, all four grandparents of the great majority of the second group were born in the United States. Thus, there was a fairly sharp distinction between the descendants of recent immigrants and the descendants of earlier immigrants. It is a commentary on the composition of our population that no less than one-third of our sample did not have a single grandparent born in the United States. Yet, like the Catholics, these people have all but caught up in socioeconomic status with the descendants of earlier immigrants. They are somewhat deficient still by way of education, but are on a par in terms of income and occupation. Yet, despite the similarity in socioeconomic status, 52 per cent of them consider themselves as Democrats, compared with only 42 per cent of those respondents some or all of whose grandparents were born in the United States.*

There are several things that can be said about these figures. In the first place, most of what has been written above about Catholics applies to the descendants of more recent immigrants in general. In fact, they tend to be much more heavily Catholic (41 per cent) than the offspring of the older stock (14 per cent), which reinforces their allegiance to the Democratic Party. Secondly, a far higher proportion of those with no grandparents born in the United States live in the East (45 per cent) and in the great metropolitan centers (47 per cent) than do the descendants of the earlier settlers (19 per cent and 24 per cent, respectively). With this kind of configuration, religious, geographic, and urban, it is not surprising that the descendants of the more recent immigrants are decidedly more liberal than the older stock on the Operational Spectrum and on the question regarding Governmental power, and less conservative on the Ideological Spectrum. This can be seen in Tables 1, 2, and 3 of Appendix F, pp. 215 ff.

These tables also show the same marked differences in degrees of liberalism and conservatism between those of Irish (Catholic), Italian, and East European or Central European origins, the majority of whom are descendants of more

* See Table 9 in Appendix F, p. 234.

recent immigrants, and those the descendants of earlier immigrants of English, German, or Scandinavian stock. To illustrate the variations involved, here are the percentages of different ethnic groups which qualified as "completely liberal" on the Operational Spectrum:

English	30%
German	34
Scandinavian	39
Irish (Catholic)	54
Eastern or Central European	54
Italian	57

The contention sometimes made that ethnic origins are no longer a significant factor in American politics is obviously not well taken, at least as of the mid-1960's. The special ethnic interests of particular groups may no longer govern their voting behavior: Poles may no longer react primarily to the Polish question or the Irish primarily to the Irish question. But there are very basic differences in outlook between the descendants of more recent immigrants and the descendants of older stock.

"Profiles" of the Two Parties

The strengths and weaknesses of the two major political parties have been discussed in terms of the population groups that compose them. But there remains the question of the relative importance of each of these groups as a potential source of votes for the Democratic and Republican parties. Table IX-12 shows the composition of the total adult population in our sample of a cross section of potential voters and the corresponding composition of the adherents of the two parties. In short, the table gives "profiles" of the total population, on the one hand, and of Democrats and Republicans, on the other. In studying these figures, we must remember that those who identified themselves as Democrats outnumbered Republicans two to one. Consequently, if the table shows that a given percentage of Democrats belongs to a certain subgroup and the same percentage of Republicans belongs to that group, in absolute terms the number of Democrats involved is twice the number of Republicans.

TABLE IX-12

PARTIES BY DEMOGRAPHIC COMPOSITION

	Total Sample	Republicans	Democrats
Age			
21–29	16%	12%	15%
30–49	44	36	46
50 & over	40	52	39
	100%	100%	100%
Education			
Grade school	33%	27%	38%
High school	48	43	48
College	19	30	14
	100%	100%	100%
Income			
Under $5,000	43%	38%	49%
$5,000–$9,999	40	36	40
$10,000 & over	17	26	11
	100%	100%	100%
Occupation			
Professional and business	23%	32%	17%
White-collar workers	10	11	9
Farmers	6	7	6
Blue-collar workers	44	31	51
Nonlabor	17	19	17
	100%	100%	100%
Union Member			
Yes	25%	15%	30%
No	75	85	70
	100%	100%	100%

TABLE IX-12 (*Continued*)

	Total Sample	Republicans	Democrats
Religion			
Protestant	71%	85%	64%
Catholic	21	11	27
Jewish	4	1	5
Other or none	4	3	4
	100%	100%	100%
City Size			
500,000 & over	34%	28%	38%
50,000–499,999	22	18	24
2,500–49,999	16	22	13
Under 2,500 & rural	28	32	25
	100%	100%	100%
Region			
East	28%	30%	30%
South	27	17	30
Midwest	29	35	25
West	16	18	15
	100%	100%	100%
Grandparents			
None born in U.S.	32%	27%	36%
Some born in U.S.	68	73	64
	100%	100%	100%
Race			
White	90%	98%	82%
Negro	10	2	18
	100%	100%	100%

The Democratic Party as shown by the make-up of its adherents is clearly a party of the "people," broadly based in
terms of all segments of the population, especially Negro
Americans and the descendants of more recent immigrant
groups. One-half of all Democrats are blue-collar workers;

one-half have annual incomes of less than $5,000; one-half have only a high school education. Two-fifths live in large metropolitan centers, where population growth has been most pronounced. In general, the Democratic Party is strongest among exactly those elements of the population which, potentially at least, have the most votes.

In contrast, the Republican Party consists almost entirely of whites, and 85 per cent of its members are Protestants. The startling fact also emerges that 52 per cent of the Republicans are fifty years of age or over. Similarly, one-half of Republican strength is located in smaller cities, towns, and rural areas, which have increasingly been losing their population to the larger centers. The party is strongest among the professional and business class, which also means among the college-educated and the well-to-do. But the professional and business people make up only one-fourth of potential voters and the college-educated and well-to-do less than one-fifth.

Against this background, it is understandable why the number of Americans who identify themselves as Republicans has declined from 38 per cent in 1940 to 29 per cent at the end of 1966 (Gallup: December 21, 1966). The Republican Party has held the Presidency for only eight out of the past thirty-four years. During that time, it has won only two Congressional elections—one in 1946 when Truman was at his low point; and, again, with Eisenhower in 1952, but then only by a one-seat majority in the Senate and a five-seat majority in the House. Despite the current euphoria in Republican ranks over the results of the 1966 elections, although the Party did much better than in 1964 and most other election years, 1966 cannot be considered a year of unqualified victory. The Republicans won the governorships of half the states, but they attracted only a minority (48.3 per cent) of the Congressional vote (as compared with the

Democrats' 51.7 per cent), and ended up with only 40 per cent of the seats in the state legislatures.

Given the rather grim history of the last three and a half decades, what about the future of the Republican Party? The 1966 election showed, at least, that the Republicans still have a good deal of vim and vigor, and, under certain conditions, voter appeal. But is the Republican Party doomed to permanent minority status, so that to win nationally it must attract the votes of most of the Independents and some of the Democrats, as well as practically all of the Republicans? As has been the case since the days of the New Deal, will a Republican victory at the national level continue to be the exception? To a great extent, the future of the Republican Party depends on how the Republicans handle the quandary discussed in the next chapter.

X

The Republican Party
and the Future

The Republican Dilemma

During the campaign of 1964, Barry Goldwater and Nelson
Rockefeller put their fingers on the basic, long-range dilemma of the Republican Party: Goldwater in his slogan,
"a choice, not an echo"; Rockefeller in his insistence that
the Party rejoin the "mainstream" of American political
thought.

From the Republican point of view, the difficulty is that
the mainstream of American politics today is represented by
the New Deal to Fair Deal to New Frontier to Great Society
trend: that is, toward the welfare state, where the majority
of Americans seem to want it to go. This movement is by
no means a consistently rapid one. At times it rushes forward, as during the early part of the Johnson Administration, when much of the Great Society program was pushed
through the Eighty-ninth Congress. At other times, as during
the Eisenhower years, the mainstream only meanders or virtually stops; it is full of backwaters and eddies. But, as with
a glacier, when there is movement it is always inexorably in
the same direction, toward the welfare state; there has never

been any real turning back, only a slowing down from time to time.

This mainstream has been decisively pre-empted by the Democratic Party. It is clear from our study that the New Deal to Great Society trend is in accord with the outlook of the vast majority of Democrats. The only sizeable group of Democrats who have been out of accord are those in the Southern states that went for Goldwater in 1964, but they make up a small minority of the national total of Democratic adherents. Apart from them, the Democratic Party has no major problem at the popular level with regard to the cohesiveness of its followers in support of this trend, even in the rest of the South, as the results on our Operational Spectrum show.

This trend also reflects the operational orientations of a majority of the American people as a whole, no matter to what ideological notions they may pay lip service. The public may approve a slowing down of the rate of flow, but it will not countenance any serious threat to the social gains already embodied in the New Deal to Great Society trend. As a result, when, for the first time in many years, Barry Goldwater offered a real choice in a Presidential election by proposing a non-mainstream (or, more aptly, anti-mainstream) alternative, he was defeated by the greatest popular landslide in any Presidential race in American history.

The Significance of Goldwater's Defeat

Goldwater supporters try to rationalize his defeat by saying the election was not a true test of the potential appeal of conservatism. They point to the fact that the assassination of President Kennedy undoubtedly hurt the Republican candidate among other ways by engendering a reaction against extremism. They charge that Goldwater's campaign was badly managed. They claim Goldwater was not an eloquent or even adequate spokesman for the conservative cause. They say he conducted himself in a way that unnecessarily frightened many voters and prejudiced them against him.

Many of these points contain elements of truth. In a special survey conducted for us by the Gallup organization, for example, when respondents were asked what they liked least about Goldwater, the item most frequently mentioned (by 17 per cent) was that he was "contradictory, inconsistent, rash; he talks too much without thinking things through"; and another response (by 7 per cent) was that he was "unreliable, untrustworthy, impulsive." To a certain extent, however, the public recognized the virtue accompanying these defects, for the leading item in the list of what they liked best about Goldwater was that he was "straightforward, forthright, honest, courageous" (mentioned by 20 per cent). Our interviewers also read a list of unfavorable charges being made by Goldwater's critics and asked whether, in the opinion of those interviewed, they were true or untrue, with the following results:

	True	*Untrue*	*Don't know*
Goldwater wants to take us back to the horse-and-buggy days.	24%	55%	21%
Goldwater would endanger the peace; he is trigger-happy.	42	38	20
Goldwater is an extremist— a radical.	46	32	22
Goldwater is too impulsive; he shoots from the hip.	60	21	19

No doubt a good many Americans were apprehensive about Goldwater. A woman in Brooklyn said: "Goldwater scares me because of his backing of extremism." A Negro in Philadelphia had this to say: "Well, if Johnson wins, things will be O.K. They say the other guy might have us go to war with Russia." The wife of a Maryland airways engineer made this comment: "Right now my main fears and worries have to do with the outcome of the election. If Goldwater is elected, you don't know what to expect. He seems too quick to speak without thinking. He might bring us closer to war." A seventy-five-year-old widow living in Wisconsin said: "I am worried about Goldwater for President. He makes so many rash statements and then has to explain them."

This reminds us of a couple of cartoons published in the *Washington Post,* among other papers, during the campaign. One, by Herblock, shows Goldwater and Eisenhower leaning over the fence at Eisenhower's farm, with Ike saying: "Criticism of you is tommyrot! Naturally you don't mean all those dopey things you've said." Another, by Parker, shows a supporter at a Goldwater rally. He is wearing earmuffs and saying: "I've made up my mind to vote for Goldwater no matter what he says!" Then there is the story of the Goldwater aide who during the New Hampshire campaign snapped at reporters: "Don't print what he *says;* print what he *means.*"

Perhaps candidate Goldwater did express himself in ways which gave the impression he was "trigger happy," an "extremist," and "impulsive," and these impressions may have cost him thousands or even hundreds of thousands of votes. But the contentions of his conservative critics overlook the main point: no genuine, thoroughgoing conservative, too far separated from the mainstream of American political thought—which is where the real conservatives want their champion to be—is likely to win a Presidential election as long as the political orientations of a large majority of

American voters remain as they are now. If some other more cautious, more discreet (and hence less engaging) conservative had been running in 1964, President Johnson's plurality might conceivably have been reduced. But, if the Republican conservative flew his true colors so it became clear that his election would threaten the social gains of the New Deal to Great Society trend, he would also have been beaten, and beaten decisively, by the Democratic contender in the mainstream of American political thought, no matter how skillfully the Republicans conducted their campaign.

In short, it is nonsense to contend that Goldwater single-handedly let the conservative cause down. The cause he represented was doomed to failure long before he even began his campaign, for the simple reason that the great majority of Americans are operational liberals who will not tolerate an out-and-out operational conservative as President. As long as Goldwater could talk ideology alone, he was able to ride high, wide, and handsome. But the moment he was forced to discuss issues and programs, he was finished— as any other true conservative would have been who opposed programs of the types popular on our Operational Spectrum. The 1964 election was really not a referendum on conflicting ideologics; it was a referendum on whether Government power and resources should continue to be used to accomplish social objectives—and the outcome was never really in doubt.

Goldwater's defeat was, of course, of staggering proportions. One out of every five Republicans deserted him (Galrup: December 11, 1964). And in no demographic group apart from the Republicans did he win a majority, not even among the normally Republican-oriented college-educated, the well-to-do, or business and professional groups.[17] Apart from his own Arizona, Barry Goldwater carried only five states in the Deep South, where the civil rights issue was the paramount motivating force.

The Conservative Minority

Yet, as his followers are fond of pointing out, Goldwater did poll over twenty-seven million votes running under the conservative banner. Considering the basic handicap under which he was operating, this seems a truly major accomplishment. The Republicans supplied about fifteen million of these votes (Gallup: December 11, 1964), but, in addition, 13 per cent of the Democrats and no less than 44 per cent of the Independents opted for Goldwater (Gallup: December 13, 1964). As would be expected, his following had a demographic pattern similar to that of Republican adherents as a whole, as shown above. Our survey and Gallup's release of December 13, 1964, show that most of those who voted for him were white Protestants. He received stronger than average support from the college-educated, almost half of whom chose him over Johnson. (The impression that Goldwater supporters were "a bunch of ignorant kooks" is ridiculous.) Support from members of the professional and business group, white-collar workers, and farmers was greater than average. He did better among old than among young people; also in localities of under 50,000 population and in the rural areas. But even with his twenty-seven million votes, he was buried under the Johnson landslide.

The essential defect in Goldwater's candidacy (which would be shared by any other true conservative) shows up in the results on our Ideological and Operational Spectrums. When the Ideological Spectrum is correlated with the "trial heat" question, in which those interviewed were asked which of the two candidates they would like to see win, Table X-1 shows that those who were "completely conservative" at the ideological level did indeed support Goldwater but even among them Johnson took four out of every ten votes. And those who were "predominantly conservative" actually opted for Johnson by more than two to one. On the whole, Johnson won about as many votes as Goldwater among ideological conservatives. Yet it was precisely among these ideological conservatives that Goldwater should have won a huge majority if the appeals of conservatism were to carry the day. However, in the case of half the ideological conservatives, the ideological appeal alone was not strong enough to control their voting behavior.

TABLE X-1

TRIAL HEAT BY IDEOLOGICAL SPECTRUM

	For Johnson	For Goldwater
Ideological Spectrum		
Completely liberal	98%	2%
Predominantly liberal	92	8
Middle of the road	89	11
Predominantly conservative	69	31
Completely conservative	38	62

The picture that emerges on the Operational Spectrum is different but equally revealing. According to Table X-2, the majority of Goldwater supporters were either conservative or middle of the road at the operational level of Government programs. But almost one-third were operational liberals. In brief, even though Goldwater was able to gain their votes, he was unable to convince one-third of his own followers that the Governmental programs he opposed were ill-advised. This reflects the broader fact that there is much less cohesion in the Republican than in the Democratic camp on this central issue, making it more difficult for Republicans to agree on platforms and programs.

TABLE X-2

TRIAL HEAT BY OPERATIONAL SPECTRUM

	For Johnson	For Goldwater
Operational Spectrum		
Completely liberal	56% ⎫ 79%	15% ⎫ 32%
Predominantly liberal	23 ⎰	17 ⎰
Middle of the road	17 } 17	30 } 30
Predominantly conservative	3 ⎫ 4	16 ⎫ 38
Completely conservative	1 ⎰	22 ⎰
	100%	100%

The essential weakness of Goldwater's conservative appeal can be put in another way. Among those who were more concerned about ideological matters than about Government programs—that is, whose score on the chart of Ideological Concerns was higher than on that of Operational Concerns—Goldwater, as would be expected, won out over Johnson by a ratio of two to one (61 per cent to 31 per cent, the rest being "don't knows" on the trial heat question). On the other hand, among those whose score on the Operational Concerns table was higher than on the Ideological, Johnson was the choice by the overwhelming ratio of 81 per cent to 14 per cent. Since, of course, far more Americans are operationally oriented than are ideologically oriented in their concerns, Johnson won by a huge majority. The lesson of the 1964 Presidential election is about as elementary as that.

This is not to say that thoroughgoing conservatives cannot be elected to state and local offices and to the United States Senate and House of Representatives. They have been in the past, both as Republicans and as Democrats, and they will no doubt continue to be in the future. But no died-in-the-wool ultra-conservative is likely to be elected President of the United States in the now-foreseeable future.[18]

Ultra-Conservatism

The ultra-conservatives and the extreme right are receiving a good deal of attention these days, much of it of an alarmist nature. The ultra-conservatives are busily organizing and winning converts and successfully infiltrating a certain number of Republican and other organizations at the state and local level in various parts of the country. But, nationally speaking, how much basis in popular support, actual or potential, does their cause enjoy under present circumstances? There are a number of ways of getting at this, all of them tangential.

We can start with the fact that even Barry Goldwater, who was not really an extremist in the John Birch Society sense, lost the 1964 election. If even he was defeated by a landslide, one can imagine what would have happened if a real ultra-conservative had been the candidate. In fact, even though the Republicans are more conservative than the Democrats, not even the milder Goldwater was the preferred choice of the great majority of Republicans when it came to nominating their standard bearer in 1964. A Gallup survey completed just prior to the Republican convention showed that the combined percentages of Republicans hoping that Lodge, Scranton, or Rockefeller, the moderates or "liberals," would get the nomination exceeded the percentage preferring Goldwater, the sole conservative, by more than two to one (Gallup: November 11, 1964). As to the election itself, after an analysis of 45,000 interviews conducted during the campaign, Harris found that "only approximately six million of the twenty-seven million who voted the Goldwater-Miller ticket can be considered hard-core, down-the-line Goldwater supporters. . . . The interviews show that an estimated eighteen million voted for the 1964 GOP nominee primarily because of Party loyalty, although expressing serious reservations about specific stands taken by Barry Goldwater. Another three million in the Goldwater column—two million Southern Democrats among them—were motivated mainly by the race issue" (Harris: January 11, 1965). After the election, only 17 per cent of registered Republicans thought Goldwater and his followers should control the Republican Party, while 70 per cent felt the Party should be controlled mostly by men with more moderate views, with 13 per cent having no opinion on the matter (Harris: April 12, 1965). Thus, despite being more conservative than the Democrats, a majority of Republicans are allergic even to that degree of conservatism represented by Goldwater, let alone to the degree propounded by the ultra-conservatives.

Two readings, at different points in time, of attitudes toward the John Birch Society, the most prominent manifestation of extreme right positions, confirm the majority aversion to ultra-conservatism. The first was the following question asked in our behalf by the Gallup Poll in December 1963 of the 69 per cent of the sample population who said they had heard or read of the John Birch Society:

> QUESTION: If you knew that a candidate for high public office was supported by the John Birch Society, would you be more likely to vote for him or less likely to vote for him?

More likely	6%
Less likely	41
Don't know	22
	69%

Later, in December 1965, the Gallup Poll asked the public to rate the John Birch Society, with these results:

Highly favorable	3%
Mildly favorable	11
Mildly unfavorable	12
Highly unfavorable	40
No opinion	34
	100%

Finally, and in some ways perhaps most directly pertinent, is the fact that only 7 per cent of Americans are completely conservative at the operational level of Government programs, the only position on the Operational Spectrum consistent with ultra-conservative doctrines. Thus, popular support for the extreme right is minimal at the present time, despite the organizational efforts that are being exerted.

Republican Strategy

If Republicans simply wanted to increase their chances of winning the Presidency by adjusting to the political orientations of the majority of the public, they would nominate a man whose views put him exactly in the mainstream of the New Deal, Great Society trend. This solution to the Republican dilemma would fail to offer "a choice, not an echo." It would also be politically impracticable. The average Republican as well as the "professional" is too conservative at heart to choose as his champion an advocate of the welfare state. Therefore, if the Republicans are to win the Presidency, they must produce a candidate conservative enough to win the nomination but not so conservative as to lose the election. The adjective most commonly used to describe such a Republican is "moderate."

Such a candidate could talk conservative ideology to his heart's content and a majority of the American people would go along with him. He could advocate slowing down the movement toward the welfare state. He could say we al-

ready have enough programs on the statute books and that
the problem now is one of consolidation and effective administration. He could advocate spending fewer Government dollars on these programs. But he must not appear to
constitute a threat to the very existence of the social programs that have emerged over the past several decades or
his fate will be the same as Barry Goldwater's. A postal employee in Pennsylvania undoubtedly reflected the thought
of the majority of Americans when, during the 1964 Presidential campaign, he expressed a fear of "reactionary leadership in our government that would repeal all our social
gains made in the last 30 years." A Florida housewife said:
"I would hate to see conservatism set back the progress of
the country. I'm a spender and a go-aheader."

In terms of platform, the most effective general posture
for a Republican candidate for the Presidency is summed
up in a slogan used by the Republican Party in Maryland in
1966: "Progress *at a pace you can afford.*" It was the Republican moderates, adopting this general approach, rather
than the outright conservatives, who accounted for most of
the major Republican victories in the Congressional and
state elections in 1966. On some such basis, the Republicans,
even though a minority party, can win the Presidency, at
least from time to time, especially when these two factors
are present: (1) popular dissatisfaction or disillusionment
with an incumbent Democratic administration and (2) the
nomination by the Republicans of a candidate who is a
moderate with an outstanding personality and a charismatic
appeal.

Future Potentialities

The fact that a fourth of the voting population consider
themselves Independents obviously provides a ready source
of votes for Republican candidates, if the right men are

nominated and favorable conditions exist. But can the Republican Party increase the proportion of its habitual adherents to such an extent that victories at the national level will no longer be rather tenuous exceptions? One of the most promising developments for Republicans in this respect is, of course, that the traditional Democratic monopoly of the Solid South appears to be breaking up. Gallup has found that almost eight out of ten Southerners think "the South would be better off, in general, if there were two political parties of about equal strength instead of one strong party as there is at present" (November 18, 1966). So far, however, the relaxation of the Democratic grip on the South has occurred primarily at the level of voting behavior rather than at the level of party identification. Goldwater won more than 47 per cent of the votes in the thirteen States that we include in the "South." * But, as of October 1966 only 15 per cent of Southerners identified themselves as "Republicans" (Gallup Political Index, Report No. 16). It may be some time before any appreciable transference of habitual psychological allegiances will occur, but such a shift is a distinct possibility in the future.

Several other trends are evident which may ultimately augment conservative orientations and thereby strengthen the Republican Party. For one thing, we are as a people becoming better educated and more affluent. On the basis of the present dispositions of the college-educated and the well-to-do, this could foreshadow a growth in conservative sentiment and Republican allegiance. It should be noted, however, that the increasing affluence of our society has so far not led to any increase in regular Republicans; in fact, just the reverse has occurred. Another factor is that automation is decreasing the proportion of the labor force in the blue-

* See p. 214 in Appendix F for the list.

collar category, where the Democrats are strongest, and increasing the proportion in the white-collar groups, among whom Republicans are at less of a disadvantage. On the other hand, the trend toward continuing population growth in the large metropolitan centers should help the Democrats, although the movement toward the suburbs within this trend may strengthen the Republicans.

But how about the young? Can the Republicans win over enough young voters to enable the party to profit eventually through the process of generational transference already described? On the surface, at least, Table X-3 would seem to suggest that this is a possibility. While the number of people who identify themselves as Republicans is no greater among those in the 21–29 age bracket than among those in the 30–49 bracket, the number of Democrats is smaller and of Independents appreciably greater. This probably reflects the fact that young people are less interested in politics and hence less likely to adopt party allegiances. Yet the proportion of Independents among the young does indicate a potential source of Republican votes. However, what is the prospect that the Republican camp can attract on a more permanent basis a substantial proportion of these three-out-of-ten younger voters who call themselves Independents? The outlook here is not encouraging for the basic reason that, on all of our measurements of liberalism and conservatism, the 21–29 age group showed almost exactly the same pattern as the group of those in their thirties and forties, rather than the more conservative pattern of people fifty and over. There are no more ideological conservatives among young people than among the middle-aged group. The proportion of operational liberals is slightly higher, and even fewer of the young (19 per cent) than of the middle-aged (26 per cent) believe that Government has too much power. The present pattern of political orientations basically favorable to Democratic allegiance will probably continue.*

TABLE X-3
PARTY IDENTIFICATIONS BY AGE

	21–29	30–49	50 and over
Identify themselves as			
Republicans	19%	20%	31%
Democrats	47	52	48
Independents	31	25	19
Other, or don't know	3	3	2
	100%	100%	100%

Change, of course, is the order of the day; and only a fool would dare predict that these basic orientations will not change as time goes on. However, in the foreseeable future, the possibility that the Republicans should again become a majority party seems relatively remote.

Philosophies and Programs

Assuming that the Republicans remain a minority party, what can they do to win more elections besides nominate attractive moderate candidates? The weakness of Republicans today is that, though they have a political philosophy, they do not have a plausible program. Their philosophy consists of the traditional American ideology which conforms to the ideological concepts of a majority of Americans. But the majority of the American people are less concerned about

* In 1966, a year generally considered unusually favorable to the Republican cause, 55 per cent of those in the 21–29 age group indicated that they were going to vote for Democratic candidates for the House of Representatives (Gallup: December 14, 1966).

ideology than about very real problems confronting their society: problems of poverty, education, transportation, air and water pollution, urban decay, race relations, and so on. Most Americans are looking for practical rather than doctrinaire solutions.

In recent times, the Republican Party has failed at the national level to put forward a program that seemed to embody constructive, viable alternatives to those offered by the Democrats, which have invariably involved a continual, increasing resort to the use of Federal power and resources. By and large, Republican response to this has been simply to oppose Democratic initiatives, particularly at the Congressional level, rather than to offer real alternatives. When the public is dissatisfied with an incumbent Democratic administration, the Republicans obviously win votes. But to be against the incumbent administration is not enough to provide a continuing Republican appeal, effective in all seasons.

At the state level, various outstanding Republican governors have devised programs which embodied constructive alternatives to the Democratic method of problem-solving. To mention only a few, La Follette in Wisconsin, Earl Warren in California, Harold Stassen in Minnesota, William Scranton in Pennsylvania, George Romney in Michigan, and Nelson Rockefeller in New York. The Republican need is to apply to the national scene the pragmatic approach these men have exercised, to devise alternative solutions, consistent with the Republican philosophy, to the Democratic one of "let Uncle Sam do it." A basic move in this direction has been made by Nelson Rockefeller in his book, *The Future of Federalism* (Cambridge: Harvard University Press, 1962), and by his continuing insistence upon state and regional, as opposed to purely Federal, solutions to the needs of society. Republicans must face the fact that their future will be bleak indeed if they cannot demonstrate they can solve national problems as well as, if not better than, the Democrats.

While Republicans have a philosophy but no program, the Democrats have a program but no philosophy. There is a real need for the Democrats to formulate a liberal political philosophy which would invest and convey the meaning of their pragmatic programs, counteract the present political schizophrenia, and transform specific objectives into examples of general principles.

As a Maryland housewife put it when asked how the country is doing domestically:

> I think it's all mixed up. I don't think it knows where it's going. I think it's very, very confused. People have lost the old rules and values by which they lived, and they haven't got any new ones to substitute.

XI

American Political Credos:
A Psychological Overview

The Basic National Assumption

The traditional political ideology in America stems from the compact signed aboard the *Mayflower* in 1620. Those who signed that document "solemnly & mutualy in the presence of God, and one of another, covenant & combine our selves togeather into a civill body politick . . ." [19] Thus seventy years before Locke's *Two Treatises on Government* and one hundred and forty-two years before Rousseau's *Social Contract,* this resolute and devout band of pilgrims was consciously expressing its desire to begin an experiment in self-government. The basic tenet of the Mayflower Compact was echoed by John Adams in 1780 when he wrote the Preamble to the Massachusetts Constitution: "The Body-Politic . . . is a social compact, by which the whole people covenants with each Citizen, and each Citizen with the whole people, that all shall be governed by certain Laws for the Common good." [20]

As Henry Steele Commager has pointed out, while Americans did not originate or invent these principles "they did something more: they institutionalized them." [21] They were the first people to specify clearly, as in their Declaration of

174

Independence, that government derives its powers from the consent of the governed, and they invented the institution of the constitutional convention to create the instruments to effect these powers.

The beginnings of the American experiment in government are of course familiar to every American school child; we recall them here because they reflect the basic political values that have shaped the American political system for nearly three hundred and fifty years. For these views represent the basic assumptions underlying the American view of life.

It is common knowledge, derived from observation and confirmed by hundreds of experiments in the psychological laboratory, that people perceive their environment in quite different ways, depending on the assumptions they bring to it. These assumptions, in turn, are built up from people's experiences in carrying out their purposes. The same "happening" in the environment will be perceived by one person as good, by another as bad; by one as progress, by another as retrogression; by one as an opportunity, by another as a threat. While perceptions, opinions, and beliefs are rooted in past experiences, they are at the same time always oriented toward the future. Indeed, perception can be thought of as a way of looking at things in the light of our hopes and expectations for the future, which in turn are based on our judgment of past experiences.

We become aware of things around us only insofar as they are related to our purposes. *At*tention depends on *in*tention. The significance of a thing to the person chiefly determines what he will learn and cling to as a belief and a loyalty. What is potentially significant in the environment is judged in terms of its effect on feelings. People obviously want to deepen and extend the range of those feelings they have enjoyed just as they want to avoid those found unpleasant or painful. Human beings are less likely than any other species on the planet to be satisfied with just any set of circumstances or conditions into which they happen to be born. Thus the development of a human being largely consists in his effort to make his environment accommodate his purposes.

While all living things tend to impose their designs on the environment, human beings—because of their greater ability to choose and to communicate, their capacity to devise, to pass on, and to alter a symbolic structure—are ceaselessly attempting to experience greater satisfactions in living as well as to protect gains already made. This leads to constant change on the personal level, which inextricably affects and is affected by change on the larger social, political, and economic scene. Thus, political behavior is an important factor in humanizing both the physical and social environment around us. The data provided in the previous chapters give ample evidence of the role of personal assumptions, based on past experiences, in creating political opinions that direct national behavior according to individual purposes and loyalties.

The assumptions engendered in the course of life develop a pattern by which we interpret the environment around us and assign characteristics to objects, to people, to words, to beliefs. It furnishes the constancies in perception by which we differentiate between what is repeatable and can be taken for granted, and what is new, changing, threatening, or emergent. This pattern of significances is our reality world, the only world we know.

Constancy and Change

Our study has shown that the underlying personal political credos of the majority of Americans have remained substantially intact at the ideological level. But the objective environment in which people live has obviously changed immeasurably. Dumas Malone, commenting on Jefferson's First Inaugural Address, noted that Jefferson pronounced his views "in an age which was not only prenuclear but which in America was virtually preindustrial. Common sense requires that allowance be made for changed circumstances; American society has been so transformed since Jefferson's inauguration that almost the only factors common to that time and this are those of topography, climate, and human nature." [22] But in concluding his essay on Jefferson's inaugural, Malone points out that "We cannot learn from him the 'how' of government, but we can learn the 'why.' " [23]

As America became an industrial power, then in recent years a nuclear power, changes occurred in human relationships and in the possibilities of acquiring satisfactions. For example, among other things, the system that obtained between whites and Negroes in the South, a sort of fealty system in which many Negroes could expect to be "taken care of," has practically disappeared; the closing of the frontier years ago and the continual increase in the size and complexity of large corporations handling the production, distribution, and communications of the nation have radically altered the possibility of being a successful, independent operator; an economy dominated by farmers and small business men has changed into one dominated by huge corporations; a rural society has become increasingly urban. Such changes have increased the impersonalness of many economic and social relationships. As a further part of this transformation, the United States has shifted its posture in recent decades from isolationism in a relatively simple world to leadership in a very complex one. As a result of this evolution, both domestic and international, Americans find themselves wrestling with relatively recent problems as apparently diverse as civil rights, job security, old age pensions, automation, world leadership, nuclear war, and the outer space race—all problems demanding modern solutions.

Within the American system, adaptation to changing conditions has taken place for nearly two hundred years—sometimes peacefully, sometimes bitterly, once with a civil war. Our study has revealed the amazing elasticity of the American experiment and the rather rapid devising and acceptance of practical programs of action to accommodate both the continuing and the emerging needs and aspirations of the nation's citizens. Because of these practical adaptations to emerging situations, the majority of the American people have never yet become so dissatisfied with their political ideology as to feel intensely and continuously frustrated. An ideology that has become part of one's self will not be thrown overboard unless frustration is deep and prolonged. Only then does despair with the current state of things set in, leading to a search for more adequate assumptions and new rallying symbols.

Political Pragmatism

In view of the discrepancy between the public's ideological and operational perceptions which our study has made crystal clear, what seems to make the American system continue to function as effectively as it does is its distinctively American pragmatism, pervading, shaping, and interpreting the American political credo. Most Americans seem determined to devise, adapt, and adopt within the framework of democracy whatever means are necessary to accommodate human feelings in greater measure. Just what human feelings and values they want to accommodate, the American people continue to insist, is for them to decide. They are not willing to turn Government over to experts. But they are willing to let trained experts work out the means of accommodation, while keeping an eagle eye on them.

For the past few decades, this accommodation has been fostered by an increase in Government power—a trend the great majority favor in practice since, to them, there seems to be no alternative to ensure human welfare and spread the bounties of a highly industrialized country rich in natural resources, a country which is, in fact, the most rapidly "developing" country on earth. People want to have, in a nation well able to afford them, the corollary benefits of more extensive education, greater health and old age benefits, more and better jobs, and other contributions to human welfare. At the same time, inconsistently and somewhat vestigially, a majority of Americans continue to cling to the traditional American ideology, which advocates the curbing of governmental power on social and domestic economic matters.

The United States is the oldest existing democracy on earth and the greatest power in the long history of man's experiments in self-government. In spite of all the differences among American citizens, they have basically a kind of Christian militancy, harking back to the Mayflower Compact and the people who cast off despotism and rank to begin an experiment in self-government. The "plain people," as Lincoln called them, have a humanitarianism that deeply respects the right of all individuals to be and to become. They have demonstrated over and over again the value they place on universal education—"The great equalizer of the conditions of men," as Horace Mann said. Such values as these—values that are deeply felt—are the moving power of American ideology, which is not to be confused with abstract ideologies.

Because of the pragmatic, humanitarian value system that characterizes the American political credo, the conflict between conservative ideologies and the liberal programs most people favor is understandable; but this divergence between theory and practice certainly spells caution, patience, and tact for any leader who counts, as he must, on continual popular support for legislation he believes will promote the public welfare. The effective leader in American democracy must of course formulate and communicate overall goals. But he must do more: he must plausibly demonstrate to a majority of citizens that the means by which he proposes to attain the goals are realistic, and at the same time he must try to persuade them that the means are not inconsistent with their basic ideological assumptions.

The American experiment has constantly been reinterpreted, readjusted, renewed, and modernized by national and political leaders, by the courts, by new legislation, and new organizations created to handle new pressures and new problems. Without such accommodation to changing circumstances, any political system either becomes outworn or loses its meaning and significance for specific situations. A viable government must remain fluid and flexible while still providing guidance and serving as a repository of accepted values.

In brief then, popular support for the American political system has persisted—and shows no signs of weakening—because that system has provided for both form and flow, the essentials for stability within change.

The Need for a Restatement of American Ideology

The paradox of a large majority of Americans qualifying as operational liberals while at the same time a majority hold to a conservative ideology has been repeatedly emphasized in this study. We have described this state of affairs as mildly schizoid, with people believing in one set of principles abstractly while acting according to another set of principles in their political behavior. But the principles according to which the majority of Americans actually behave politically have not yet been adequately formulated in modern terms. As already indicated, it is only because the American system has demonstrated such flexibility and such a capacity to accommodate to new situations that this schizoid state has not more seriously impeded the operation and direction of government.

There is little doubt that the time has come for a restatement of American ideology to bring it in line with what the great majority of people want and approve. Such a statement, with the right symbols incorporated, would focus people's wants, hopes, and beliefs, and provide a guide and platform to enable the American people to implement their political desires in a more intelligent, direct, and consistent manner.

Such a restatement would also help people throughout the world understand what the American way of life involves and what values guide it. As it is now, people outside our borders find it difficult to reconcile with our traditional, conservative ideology our government's vast program of social legislation and the international obligations it has assumed.

History shows that the great documents and teachings that have captured people's imaginations and given them new meanings on which to base action are always expressed in highly idealistic terms. But it is such idealistic documents and teachings, including those of American spokesmen in earlier days, that prove to be the height of realism, inspiring people as they do to practical achievements in a wide variety of circumstances. The statement needed today must measure no less.

APPENDICES

A

The Samples

The two samples which yielded the main data for our study were probability samples down to the block level in urban areas and to segments of townships in rural areas. They were designed to produce cross sections of the total civilian population of the United States twenty-one years of age and over, with all elements of the population represented in their proper proportion except for persons in institutions, such as prisons and hospitals. The demographic composition of the combined samples is given in the "Total Sample" column in Table IX-12, p. 153. The number of persons the interviewers questioned in the first sample was 1,611 and in the second sample 1,564.

The sample design provided for stratifying the population of the United States in two ways. First, the country was divided into seven geographic regions. Then each of these regions was subdivided on the basis of the following seven categories having to do with size of communities according to the 1960 Census: central cities with populations of 1,000,000 or more; of 250,000 to 999,999; and of 50,000 to 249,999; the urbanized areas around these central cities (*i.e.,* the suburbs); cities of 2,500 to 49,999 population; rural villages; and rural open areas. This division by region and community size thus yielded forty-nine different strata. Each of these strata was assigned that proportion of the total interviews which its population bore to the total adult population of the United States. The sampling points (that is, clusters of blocks or segments of townships) where interviews were to be conducted within each of these strata and the particular dwelling units where the interviewers were to seek out respondents at these sampling points were chosen by a process of random selection. Thus the choice of respondents was determined by an objective selection procedure narrowed down to individual dwelling units, not according to the judgment of the interviewers.

Interviewing was conducted at 160 sampling points throughout the United States in the first sample and at 169 in the second sample.

B

Questions and Overall Results

(As explained in Chapter I, our survey involved two questionnaires administered to two separate but similar samples described in Appendix A, the first consisting of 1,611 cases—i.e., interviews—the second of 1,564. A goodly number of key questions were asked of both samples, so that the total number of persons interviewed came to 3,215. The questions listed below include those asked in either or both samples, with the number of interviews on which the results are based being indicated at the end of each question. The interviewing of the first sample was conducted during the latter part of September and the beginning of October 1964; the interviewing of the second sample during the latter half of October 1964.)

1. Some people say that human nature is basically bad and that you can't be too careful in your dealings with people. Others say that human nature is basically good and that people can be trusted. From your own experience, do you think human nature is basically good or basically bad? (3,215 cases)

Good, 67%   Bad, 6%   Both good and bad, 25%
Don't know, 2%

2a. All of us want certain things out of life. When you think about what really matters in your own life, what are your wishes and hopes for the future? In other words, if you imagine your future in the *best* possible light, what would your life look like, if you are to be happy? (1,611 cases)

Take your time in answering; such things aren't easy to put into words.

(PERMISSIBLE PROBES: What are your hopes for the future? What would your life have to be like for you to be completely happy? What is missing for you to be happy?)

What other wishes and hopes do you have for the future?

(For the results, see Table VII-1, p. 97.)

2b. Now, taking the other side of the picture, what are your fears and worries about the future? In other words, if you imagine your future in the *worst* possible light, what would your life look like then? (1,611 cases)

(PERMISSIBLE PROBES: What would make you unhappy? Stress the words "fears" and "worries.")

What other fears and worries do you have about the future?

(For the results, see Table VII-2, p. 97.)

3a. (HAND RESPONDENT CARD SHOWING LADDER.) Here is a ladder symbolic of the "ladder of life." [The steps on the ladder were numbered from zero at the bottom to ten at the top.] Let's suppose the top of the ladder (POINTING) represents the *best* possible life for you; and the bottom (POINTING) represents the *worst* possible life for you. On which step of the ladder (MOVING FINGER RAPIDLY UP AND DOWN LADDER) do you feel you personally stand at the present time? (1,611 cases)

3b. On which step would you say you stood five years ago? (1,611 cases)

3c. Just as your best guess, on which step do you think you will be five years from now? (1,611 cases)

(For all three ladder ratings, see Table 7, pp. 229 f., in Appendix F.)

4a. Now, what are your wishes and hopes for the future of the United States? If you picture the future of the U.S. in the *best* possible light, how would things look, let us say, about ten years from now? (3,215 cases)

What other wishes and hopes do you have for the U.S.?

(For the results, see Table VII-6, p. 104.)

4b. And what about your fears and worries for the future of our country? If you picture the future of the U.S. in the *worst* possible light, how would things look about ten years from now? (3,215 cases)

What other fears and worries do you have about the U.S.?

(For the results, see Table VII-7, p. 105.)

5a. Looking at the ladder again, suppose the top represents the *very best* situation for our country; the bottom, the *very worst* situation for our country. Please show me on which step of the ladder you think the United States is at the present time. (1,611 cases)

5b. On which step would you say the U.S. was *five years ago*— that is, toward the end of the Eisenhower Administration? (1,611 cases)

5c. Now, looking a decade ahead, just as your best guess where do you think the U.S. will be on the ladder *ten* years from now if everything goes as you expect? (1,611 cases)

(For all three ladder ratings, see Table 8, pp. 231 ff., in Appendix F.)

6. Now, let's turn to some current issues. A broad general program of Federal aid to education is under consideration, which would include Federal grants to help pay teachers' salaries. Would you be *for* or *against* such a program? (3,215 cases)

For, 62%   Against, 28%   Don't know, 10%

7. Congress has been considering a compulsory medical insurance program covering hospital and nursing home care for
the elderly. This Medicare program would be financed out of
increased social security taxes. In general, do you *approve* or
disapprove of this program? (3,215 cases)

Approve, 63%   Disapprove, 30%   Don't know, 7%

8. Under the Federal housing program, the Federal Government is making grants to help build low-rent public housing.
Do you think Government spending for this purpose should be
kept at least at the present level, or reduced, or ended altogether?
(3,215 cases)

Present level (or increased), 63%   Reduced, 12%
Ended, 10%   Don't know, 15%

9. Under the urban renewal program, the Federal Government is making grants to help rebuild run-down sections of our
cities. Do you think Government spending for this purpose
should be kept at least at the present level, or reduced, or ended
altogether? (3,215 cases)

Present level (or increased), 67%   Reduced, 10%
Ended, 11%   Don't know, 12%

10. Now, I'm going to read some things you sometimes hear
people say, and ask whether, in general, you agree or disagree.

a. Generally speaking, any able-bodied person who really wants
   to work in this country can find a job and earn a living.
   (1,611 cases)

   Agree, 76%   Disagree, 21%   Don't know, 3%

b. Labor unions should be subject to *more* government controls and regulations. (1,611 cases)

   Agree, 52%   Disagree, 30%   Don't know, 18%

c. The Federal Government has a responsibility to try to reduce unemployment. (3,215 cases)

   Agree, 75%   Disagree, 18%   Don't know, 7%

d. The Federal Government has a responsibility to try to do away with poverty in this country. (3,215 cases)

   Agree, 72%   Disagree, 20%   Don't know, 8%

e. The Federal Government is interfering too much in state and local matters. (1,611 cases)

   Agree, 40%   Disagree, 47%   Don't know, 13%

f. The government has gone too far in regulating business and interfering with the free enterprise system. (1,611 cases)

   Agree, 42%   Disagree, 39%   Don't know, 19%

g. The government is interfering too much with property rights. (1,611 cases)

   Agree, 39%   Disagree, 37%   Don't know, 24%

h. There is too much Communist and left-wing influence in our government these days. (1,611 cases)

   Agree, 47%   Disagree, 30%   Don't know, 23%

i. We should rely more on individual initiative and ability and not so much on governmental welfare programs. (1,611 cases)

   Agree, 79%   Disagree, 12%   Don't know, 9%

j. Social problems here in this country could be solved more effectively if the government would only keep its hands off and let people in local communities handle their own problems in their own ways. (1,611 cases)

   Agree, 49%   Disagree, 38%   Don't know, 13%

k. The relief rolls are loaded with chiselers and people who just don't want to work. (1,564 cases)

   Agree, 66%   Disagree, 23%   Don't know, 11%

l. There is a definite trend toward socialism in this country. (1,564 cases)

   Agree, 46%   Disagree, 22%   Don't know, 32%

m. Welfare relief programs are needed *at the local level* so that no one will be without the necessities of life. (1,564 cases)

Agree, 86%   Disagree, 6%   Don't know, 8%

11. In your opinion, which is generally more often to blame if a person is poor—lack of effort on his own part, or circumstances beyond his control? (1,611 cases)

Lack of effort, 34%   Circumstances, 25%   Both, 38%
Don't know, 3%

12. Which one of the statements listed on this card comes closest to your own views about Governmental power today? (3,215 cases)

The Federal Government today has too much power	26%
The Federal Government is now using just about the right amount of power for meeting today's needs	36
The Federal Government should use its powers even more vigorously to promote the well-being of all segments of the people	31
Don't know	7

13. Our Federal Government, as you know, is made up of three branches: the Executive branch, headed by the President; the Judicial branch, headed by the U.S. Supreme Court; and the Legislative branch, made up of the U.S. Senate and House of Representatives. (HAND CARD SHOWING LADDER TO RESPONDENT.) I'd like you to show me on this ladder how much trust and confidence you have in each of these branches, under present circumstances. [The steps on the ladder were numbered from zero at the bottom to ten at the top.] The top of the ladder in this case means *the greatest possible confidence;* the bottom, *no confidence at all.* (1,611 cases)

a. First, how much trust and confidence do you have in the Executive branch, headed by the President?

Average rating, 7.43

b. Secondly, in the Judicial branch, headed by the U.S. Supreme Court?

Average rating, 6.89

c. And, finally, in the Legislative branch, made up of the Senate and House of Representatives?

Average rating, 7.23

14. In general, how much trust and confidence do you have in the wisdom of the American people when it comes to making political decisions—a very great deal, a good deal, not very much, or none at all? (1,611 cases)

Great deal	14%	Not very much	19%
Good deal	62%	None at all	1%
	Don't know	4%	

15. Thinking of people now living who are *successful* in life, which three things among those listed on this card do you feel have been chiefly responsible for their success? Just indicate the three you think are most important. (1,611 cases)

Native intelligence and ability	35%
Born into well-to-do family which gave them better opportunities	23
Good luck, getting the breaks	18
Character, will power	59
Ruthlessness, clawing their way to the top	5
Good education and training	71
Initiative and effort, hard work	66
Knew the right people, had "pull"	13
Don't know	3

16. Turning to people now living who are *unsuccessful* in life, which three things among those listed on this card do you feel are chiefly responsible for holding them back? (1,611 cases)

Unfavorable family background	17%
Lack of native intelligence and ability	32
Lack of education and training	76
Too considerate of others to stand up for their own self-interest	7
Bad luck, not getting the breaks	16
Race or religion	14
Lack of character and will power	47
Laziness, little or no ambition	57
Limited opportunities	25
Don't know	3

17. Now I'm going to mention certain groups and organizations. Please tell me whether you would like to see them have *more* influence in government and political matters than they have now, or *less* influence than they have now. If you don't know enough about some of the less familiar groups I mention, please say so. (1,564 cases)

a. First, what about labor unions? Would you like to see them have more influence or less influence?

> More, 17%   Less, 49%   About right now, 20%
> Don't know, 14%

b. Large business corporations?

> More, 12%   Less, 43%   About right now, 25%
> Don't know, 20%

c. The Negroes?

> More, 30%   Less, 31%   About right now, 28%
> Don't know, 11%

d. The Protestants?

More, 25%   Less, 7%   About right now, 49%
Don't know, 19%

e. The Jews?

More, 8%   Less, 20%   About right now, 47%
Don't know, 25%

f. The John Birch Society?

More, 3%   Less, 44%   About right now, 6%
Don't know, 47%

g. Americans for Democratic Action?

More, 11%   Less, 19%   About right now, 12%
Don't know, 58%

h. The Roman Catholics?

More, 9%   Less, 24%   About right now, 47%
Don't know, 20%

i. The American Legion?

More, 27%   Less, 10%   About right now, 39%
Don't know, 24%

18. During the past ten years there have been a number of corporations that have done more than a billion dollars' worth of business each year. Which of the four statements listed on this card comes closest to describing your own feeling about a corporation that does that much business? (1,564 cases)

It is dangerous for the welfare of the country for any companies to be this big and they should be broken up into smaller companies.   13%

While it may be necessary to have some very large companies, we should watch their activities very closely and discourage their growth as much as possible.   17

There may be some reasons against having such

large companies, but on the whole they do more
good than harm to the country. 31%

It is foolish to worry about a company just because
it is big; large companies have made America the
kind of country it is today. 29

Don't know. 10

19. As you know, a civil rights law was recently passed by
Congress and signed by the President. In general, do you *approve* or *disapprove* of this law? (3,215 cases)

Approve, 60%   Disapprove, 29%   Don't know, 11%

20. On the whole, do you think that racial integration of
Negroes in this country is going ahead *too fast* or *not fast
enough?* (1,564 cases)

Too fast, 56%   Not fast enough, 18%   About right, 20%
Don't know, 6%

21. In your opinion, are the Negroes who have been participating in the recent rioting and violence chiefly just bad characters without respect for law and order, or are they victims of despair and lack of opportunity? (1,611 cases)

Bad characters, 37%   Victims of despair, 25%
Both, neither, or other, 32%   Don't know, 6%

22. And now, one more statement: Most of the organizations
pushing for civil rights have been infiltrated by the Communists
and are now dominated by Communist trouble-makers. Do you
agree with that statement or not? (1,611 cases)

Agree, 47%   Disagree, 33%   Don't know, 20%

23. How much danger do you think the Communists right
here in America are to this country at the present time—a very
great deal, a good deal, not very much, or none at all? (1,611
cases)

Great deal	28%	Not very much	29%
Good deal	34%	None at all	3%
	Don't know	6%	

24. Is it your impression that the strength of U.S. defense is about right at present, or do you feel that it should be either increased or decreased? (1,564 cases)

About right, 52%　　Increased, 31%　　Decreased, 4%
Don't know, 13%

25. Now, some questions on international matters. First, please read all the statements on this card; and then I'm going to ask you to tell me whether you agree or disagree with each of them. (3,215 cases)

a. The U.S. should cooperate fully with the United Nations.

Agree, 72%　　Disagree, 16%　　Don't know, 12%

b. In deciding its foreign policies, the U.S. should take into account the views of its allies in order to keep our alliances strong.

Agree, 81%　　Disagree, 7%　　Don't know, 12%

c. Since the U.S. is the most powerful nation in the world, we should go our own way in international matters, not worrying too much about whether other countries agree with us or not.

Agree, 19%　　Disagree, 70%　　Don't know, 11%

d. The U.S. should mind its own business internationally and let other countries get along as best they can on their own.

Agree, 18%　　Disagree, 70%　　Don't know, 12%

e. The U.S. should maintain its dominant position as the world's most powerful nation at all costs, even going to the very brink of war if necessary.

Agree, 56%　　Disagree, 31%　　Don't know, 13%

f. We shouldn't think so much in *international* terms but concentrate more on our own *national* problems and building up our strength and prosperity here at home.

Agree, 55%　　Disagree, 32%　　Don't know, 13%

26. Now, continuing on international questions, I'm going to read you several more statements and ask you whether, in general, you agree or disagree.

a. President Johnson and his administration have been following a defeatist "no win" policy on the international front by appeasing the Communists. (1,611 cases)

    Agree, 27%   Disagree, 52%   Don't know, 21%

b. The U.S. should continue to negotiate with the Soviet Union on a broad front in the hope of reaching agreements which would contribute to world peace. (3,215 cases)

    Agree, 85%   Disagree, 7%   Don't know, 8%

c. In particular, the U.S. should continue to negotiate with Russia with a view to reducing armaments on both sides. (1,611 cases)

    Agree, 70%   Disagree, 19%   Don't know, 11%

d. The U.S. should take a firmer stand against the Soviet Union than it has in recent years. (1,611 cases)

    Agree, 61%   Disagree, 25%   Don't know, 14%

e. The U.S. should seek to roll back the Iron Curtain and liberate the satellite countries from Soviet control even if this might provoke Russia to go to war. (1,611 cases)

    Agree, 20%   Disagree, 59%   Don't know, 21%

f. No matter what the U.S. does, the Russian leaders won't risk launching a nuclear war. (1,611 cases)

    Agree, 28%   Disagree, 52%   Don't know, 20%

27. Now, let's think of the image—or picture—that people in other countries have of the U.S. From what you have heard or read, do you think U.S. prestige abroad is *high* or *low* at the present time? *Very* high (low) or only *somewhat* high (low)? (1,611 cases)

Very high	12%	Somewhat low	32%
Somewhat high	40%	Very low	7%
	Don't know	9%	

28. Can you tell me who the following people are? (1,611 cases)

	Correct
Earl Warren	63%
U Thant	40
Charles de Gaulle	71
William Fulbright	31
Ludwig Erhard	36
Sukarno	14

29a. Have you heard or read of the North Atlantic Treaty Organization—NATO, that is? (1,611 cases)

Yes, 72%   No or don't know, 28%

29b. (IF "YES") I'd like to ask you whether several countries are members of NATO or not.

	Correct
First, is the U.S. a member?	(Yes) 58%
How about Russia—is it a member?	(No) 38
And Sweden?	(No) 21

30. Under present circumstances, which countries of the world do you think it most important for the U.S. to cooperate with *very closely*? (1,564 cases)

(For the results, see Table VI-4, p. 71.)

31. And now what about economic aid to foreign countries? Do you think Government spending for this purpose should be kept at least at the present level, or reduced, or ended altogether? (1,611 cases)

Present level (or increased), 32%   Reduced, 44%
Ended, 15%   Don't know, 9%

32. In general, are you satisfied or dissatisfied with the way the U.S. Government is handling the problem of Vietnam? Very or only somewhat satisfied (dissatisfied)? (1,611 cases)

Very satisfied	7%	Somewhat dissatis-	
Somewhat satis-		fied	23%
fied	30%	Very dissatisfied	17%
	Don't know	23%	

33. There would seem to be three basic courses the U.S. could follow in Vietnam. On balance, which one of these courses [listed on a card] would you favor? (1,611 cases)

Pull out entirely	16%
Keep on about the way we have been	37
Step up the war by carrying the fight to North Vietnam, through more air strikes against Communist territory	29
Don't know	18

34. Some people say the U.S. should use stronger measures in dealing with the Cuban problem, including a naval blockade to stop military supplies from going into Cuba, or from Cuba to other countries for purposes of subversion. Other people say such measures are unnecessary and would be dangerous because they would risk a major war. How do you feel about this— would you *favor* or *oppose* stronger measures, including a naval blockade, under present circumstances? (1,611 cases)

Favor, 47%   Oppose, 34%   Don't know, 19%

35. Do you think it would be in the interests of the U.S. to establish diplomatic relations with Communist China within the next five years or not? (1,564 cases)

Would be, 36%   Would not be, 39%   Don't know, 25%

36. Which do you think will turn out to be the greater threat to the U.S.—Soviet Russia or Communist China? (1,564 cases)

Russia, 19%   China, 54%   Both equally, 18%
Don't know, 9%

37. Now, I'd like to find out how *worried* or *concerned* you are about each of the problems I am going to mention. If you don't really feel very much concerned about some of them, don't hesitate to say so. (1,564 cases)

a. First, let's take Negro racial problems. Are you concerned about these problems a great deal, considerably, not very much, or not at all?

Great deal	34%	Not very much	25%
Considerably	35%	Not at all	5%
Don't know	1%		

b. The problem of improving our educational system?

Great deal	46%	Not very much	16%
Considerably	35%	Not at all	2%
Don't know	1%		

c. Problems of labor and labor-management relations?

Great deal	22%	Not very much	32%
Considerably	34%	Not at all	4%
Don't know	6%		

d. Preserving our individual liberties against government interference?

Great deal	39%	Not very much	24%
Considerably	26%	Not at all	5%
Don't know	6%		

e. Government spending?

Great deal	35%	Not very much	23%
Considerably	35%	Not at all	4%
Don't know	3%		

f. Raising moral standards in this country?

Great deal	53%	Not very much	13%
Considerably	29%	Not at all	2%
Don't know	3%		

g. Medicare for the elderly?

Great deal	38%	Not very much	23%
Considerably	33%	Not at all	4%
Don't know	2%		

h. Preserving our free enterprise system?

Great deal	36%	Not very much	19%
Considerably	33%	Not at all	3%
Don't know	9%		

i. Unemployment in the U.S.?

Great deal	41%	Not very much	19%
Considerably	36%	Not at all	2%
Don't know	2%		

j. The problem of maintaining law and order?

Great deal	54%	Not very much	11%
Considerably	32%	Not at all	2%
Don't know	1%		

k. The trend toward a more powerful Federal Government?

Great deal	28%	Not very much	31%
Considerably	27%	Not at all	7%
Don't know	7%		

l. Reducing poverty in this country?

Great deal	37%	Not very much	18%
Considerably	39%	Not at all	3%
Don't know	3%		

m. Preserving states' rights?

Great deal	31%	Not very much	27%
Considerably	28%	Not at all	6%
Don't know	8%		

n. Keeping the country out of war?

Great deal	75%	Not very much	5%
Considerably	18%	Not at all	1%
Don't know	1%		

o. Keeping our military defense strong?

Great deal	59%	Not very much	7%
Considerably	31%	Not at all	1%
Don't know	2%		

p. Combatting world Communism?

Great deal	64%	Not very much	7%
Considerably	25%	Not at all	1%
Don't know	3%		

q. Relations with Russia?

Great deal	43%	Not very much	14%
Considerably	37%	Not at all	3%
Don't know	3%		

r. The problem of Vietnam?

Great deal	36%	Not very much	17%
Considerably	33%	Not at all	3%
Don't know	11%		

s. Strengthening the United Nations?

Great deal	28%	Not very much	24%
Considerably	35%	Not at all	6%
Don't know	7%		

t. The problem of Communist China?

Great deal	42%	Not very much	15%
Considerably	34%	Not at all	3%
Don't know	6%		

u. Keeping NATO and our other alliances strong?

Great deal	29%	Not very much	19%
Considerably	38%	Not at all	3%
	Don't know	11%	

v. Controlling the use of nuclear weapons?

Great deal	57%	Not very much	8%
Considerably	29%	Not at all	2%
	Don't know	4%	

w. Maintaining respect for the U.S. in other countries?

Great deal	54%	Not very much	9%
Considerably	31%	Not at all	2%
	Don't know	4%	

38a. Now, let's turn to some questions about politics. Which one of the words or statements listed on this card best describes President Johnson, in your opinion? (3,215 cases)

Very liberal	18%	Moderately con-	
Moderately liberal	29%	servative	10%
Middle of the		Very conservative	5%
road	29%	Don't know	9%

38b. And which describes Senator Goldwater, in your opinion? (3,215 cases)

Very liberal	5%	Moderately con-	
Moderately liberal	6%	servative	22%
Middle of the		Very conservative	28%
road	16%	Don't know	23%

38c. And how would you describe yourself? (3,215 cases)

Very liberal	6%	Moderately con-	
Moderately liberal	21%	servative	25%
Middle of the		Very conservative	7%
road	35%	Don't know	6%

38d. And how would you describe your father, politically? (3,215 cases)

Very liberal	20%	Moderately con-	
Moderately liberal	28%	servative	16%
Middle of the road	26%	Very conservative	10%

39a. Suppose the presidential election were being held to-day. Which candidate would you like to see win—Lyndon Johnson, the Democrat, or Barry Goldwater, the Republican? (3,215 cases)

39b. (IF "OTHER" OR "UNDECIDED") Well, as of today, do you lean more to Johnson, the Democrat, or to Goldwater, the Republican?

Total of *a* and *b*: *

Johnson, 66%   Goldwater, 27%   Undecided, 7%

40. In politics as of today, do you consider yourself a Republican, Democrat, or Independent? (3,215 cases)

Republican, 24%   Democrat, 49%   Independent, 24%
Other or don't know, 3%

41a. As you remember it, for which party did your father usually vote in Presidential elections when you were too young to vote? (3,215 cases)

Republican	26%	Sometimes Repub-	
Democratic	47%	lican, sometimes	
Other	1%	Democratic	6%
	Don't know	20%	

41b. And your mother—for which party did she usually vote in Presidential elections when you were too young to vote? (3,215 cases)

* These figures obviously varied considerably from the actual election results, the reason being that they represented the total adult population, including a considerable proportion of people who were unlikely to (and, in fact, did not) vote.

Republican	22%	Sometimes Repub-	
Democratic	44%	lican, sometimes	
Other	2%	Democratic	5%
Don't know	27%		

42a. Can you tell me the name of the man who is running for Vice President on the *Republican* ticket in the present campaign? (1,611 cases)

Miller, 74%   Incorrect or don't know, 26%

42b. And the name of the man who is running for Vice President on the *Democratic* ticket this time? (1,611 cases)

Humphrey, 79%   Incorrect or don't know, 21%

42c. Who ran with *Nixon* as the Vice-Presidential candidate on the *Republican* ticket in 1960? (1,611 cases)

Lodge, 31%   Incorrect or don't know, 69%

43. If anything should happen to President Johnson before the elections this November, do you happen to know who would succeed him and serve out his present term as President, as the law now stands? (1,611 cases)

Speaker of the House (or McCormack), 47%
Incorrect or don't know, 53%

44. In the field of politics and government do you feel your own interests are similar to the interests of the propertied class, the middle class, or the working class? (1,611 cases)

Propertied, 5%   Middle, 37%   Working, 53%
Don't know, 5%

(In addition, a number of standard demographic questions were asked of each respondent about his education, income, occupation, religion, ethnic origins, etc., the results of which can be found in the "Total Sample" column of Table IX-12, pp. 153 f.)

C

Operational Spectrum

Our Operational Spectrum was based on five questions—dealing with Federal aid to education, Medicare, the Federal housing program, the urban renewal program, and the Government's responsibility to do away with poverty—listed on pages 13 through 15.

The first step in tabulating was to eliminate from consideration all interviews in which respondents answered "don't know" to three or more of these questions; in other words, to be rated on the Operational Spectrum, at least three questions had to be answered either pro or con. This resulted in the elimination of 174 interviews. The remaining 3,041 cases were then divided into five categories: completely liberal, predominantly liberal, middle of the road, predominantly conservative, and completely conservative.

To qualify as "completely liberal," a respondent had to answer affirmatively all five of the questions, or four (with one "don't know"), or three (with two "don't knows")—that is, had to approve (unless undecided about) Federal aid to education, Medicare, at least the present level of Government spending for public housing and urban renewal, and agree (unless, again, he could not decide) that the Government has a responsibility to do away with poverty, but he could be undecided about no more than two of the items. Those denominated "predominantly liberal" conformed to this pattern in the case of four out of the five questions (if they answered all five), of three out of four (if they replied "don't know" on one of them), or at least of two out of three (if they answered "don't know" to two of them).

To qualify as "completely conservative," a respondent had to follow a pattern exactly the reverse of the "completely liberal" one. Those designated "predominantly conservative" conformed to this "completely conservative" pattern in the same degree that the "predominantly liberal" respondents followed the "completely liberal" pattern.

The remaining cards showing greater deviation from both the "completely liberal" and the "completely conservative" patterns were put into the "middle of the road" category, since these respondents exhibited neither consistently liberal nor consistently conservative outlooks.

D

Ideological Spectrum

Our Ideological Spectrum was based on reactions to five statements listed on pages 31 and 32. The first step in tabulating was to eliminate from consideration all interviews in which respondents answered "don't know" to three or more of these questions; in other words, an interviewee, to be rated on the Ideological Spectrum, had to react either affirmatively or negatively to at least three of the statements. This eliminated 120 interviews, leaving 1,491 cases to be divided into five categories ranging from "completely conservative" to "completely liberal."

To qualify as "completely conservative," a respondent had to agree with all five of the statements, or four (with one "don't know"), or three (with two "don't knows"). Those denominated "predominantly conservative" agreed to four out of five of the statements (if they reacted to all five), to three out of four (if one of the answers was "don't know"), or at least to two out of three (if two of the answers were "don't know").

The "completely liberal" category was exactly the reverse of the "completely conservative"—that is, all reactions given took the form of disagreement. The "predominantly liberal" group conformed to this liberal pattern in the same degree that the "predominantly conservative" respondents followed the "completely conservative" pattern.

The remaining cards showing greater deviation from both the "completely conservative" and the "completely liberal" patterns were put into the "middle of the road" category.

E

International Patterns

Our system of International Patterns was based on reactions to the following five statements:

1. The U.S. should cooperate fully with the United Nations.
2. In deciding its foreign policies, the U.S. should take into account the views of its allies in order to keep our alliances strong.
3. Since the U.S. is the most powerful nation in the world, we should go our own way in international matters, not worrying too much about whether other countries agree with us or not.
4. The U.S. should mind its own business internationally and let other countries get along as best they can on their own.
5. We shouldn't think so much in international terms but should concentrate more on our own national problems and building up our strength and prosperity here at home.

In tabulating, we eliminated from consideration 274 interviews in which respondents answered "don't know" to three or more of these questions. The remaining 2,941 cases, where answers were given to at least three of the statements, were then divided into five categories ranging from "completely internationalist" to "completely isolationist."

To qualify as "completely internationalist," a respondent had to react—whether to all five of the statements, or to four (with one "don't know"), or to three (with two "don't knows," the maximum number allowed)—by agreeing (when not undecided) that the United States should cooperate with the United Nations and take into account the views of its allies, and disagreeing that the United States should go its own way, mind its own business, and concentrate more on national problems. Those denominated "predominantly internationalist" conformed to this pattern in the case of four out of five statements (if all of them were reacted to), to three out of four (if one reply was "don't know"), or at least to two out of three (if two answers were "don't know").

The "completely isolationist" category was exactly the reverse of the "completely internationalist" one. The "predominantly isolationist" respondents conformed to the "completely isolationist" pattern in the same degree that the "predominantly internationalist" group conformed to the "completely internationalist" pattern.

The remaining cards showing greater deviation from both the "completely internationalist" and the "completely isolationist" patterns were put into the "mixed" category.

F

Tables

Abbreviations

In the following tables, these abbreviations are used: "lib." for liberal; "cons." for conservative; "compl." for completely; "pred." for predominantly; "mod." for moderately; "oper." for operational; "ideol." for ideological; "inter." for internationalist; "isol." for isolationist.

Explanation of Breakdowns

A goodly number of the breakdowns are self-explanatory. However, some require elucidation. For example, in the case of the breakdown by *education*, "grade school" includes those who have had some grade school education but have not graduated as well as those who have graduated, and similarly for "high school" and "college." *Income* is based on the total earnings of the family as a whole (that is, those members living together in the dwelling where the interview was conducted). *Class identification* was obtained by asking the following question: "In the field of politics and government do you feel your interests are similar to the interests of the propertied class, the middle class, or the working class?"

The *occupation* categories are clear except for "non-labor." This category consists primarily of households headed by retired people, and, to a lesser extent, by housewives, students, or the physically handicapped. One of its chief peculiarities is that, in our sample, 85 per cent of those in this category were fifty years of age or over; the national average for this age group was 40 per cent of the adult population. The "yes" category under *union member* includes not only people who themselves belong to labor unions but also the spouses of union members who happened to be included in the sample.

The different categories under *region* include the following states:

East: Connecticut, Maine, Massachusetts, New Hampshire, Rhode Island, Vermont, Delaware, Maryland, New Jersey, New York, Pennsylvania, West Virginia, and the District of Columbia

Midwest: Illinois, Indiana, Michigan, Ohio, Iowa, Kansas, Minnesota, Missouri, Nebraska, North Dakota, South Dakota, Wisconsin

South—Goldwater (The Southern States that gave Goldwater a majority in 1964): Alabama, Georgia, Louisiana, Mississippi, and South Carolina

South—Johnson (The Southern States that went for Johnson in 1964): Arkansas, Florida, Kentucky, North Carolina, Oklahoma, Tennessee, Texas, and Virginia

West: Arizona, Colorado, Idaho, Montana, Nevada, New Mexico, Utah, Wyoming, California, Oregon, Washington, Alaska, and Hawaii

In the case of the *grandparents* category, the distinction is between those white respondents (Negroes were excluded as constituting a separate ethnic group all to themselves) none of whose grandparents were born in the United States (so that they belong to the more recent waves of immigration) and those who had from one to four grandparents born here. Under *ethnic groups,* a respondent was classified as of a given origin (e.g., Italian) if either of his parents or their ancestors were born in the geographical area of origin. The "Irish" category refers to Irish Catholics, excluding the descendants of the Protestant Scotch-Irish. The differentiation by *party* was based on the question, "In politics as of today do you consider yourself a Republican, Democrat, or Independent?"

The trial heat results are based on these two questions:

"Suppose the Presidential election were being held today. Which candidate would you like to see win—Lyndon Johnson, the Democrat, or Barry Goldwater, the Republican?"

(IF "OTHER" OR "UNDECIDED") "Well, as of today, do you lean more to Johnson, the Democrat, or to Goldwater, the Republican?"

The *Operational Spectrum* is explained in Appendix C (p. 207); the *Ideological Spectrum* in Appendix D (p. 209); *International Patterns* in Appendix E (p. 211). The question for the table on Government power read as follows:

"Which one of the statements listed on this card comes closest to your own views about Governmental power today?

a. The Federal Government today has too much power.
b. The Federal Government is now using just about the right amount of power for meeting today's needs.
c. The Federal Government should use its powers even more vigorously to promote the well-being of all segments of the people."

In the case of the *self-identification* category, respondents were asked whether they described themselves politically as being very liberal, moderately liberal, middle of the road, moderately conservative, or very conservative.

TABLE 1

OPERATIONAL SPECTRUM

	Compl. Lib.	Pred. Lib.	Middle of Road	Pred. Cons.	Compl. Cons.
National Totals	44%	21%	21%	7%	7%
Sex					
Male	42	21	22	8	7
Female	45	22	19	7	7

TABLE 1 (*Continued*)

	Compl. Lib.	Pred. Lib.	Middle of Road	Pred. Cons.	Compl. Cons.
Age					
21–29	47%	22%	23%	5%	3%
30–49	44	23	20	7	6
50 & over	42	19	21	9	9
Education					
Grade school	54	21	16	6	3
High school	42	23	22	6	7
College	32	19	24	12	13
Income					
Under $5,000	52	21	16	6	5
$5,000–$9,999	41	21	24	7	7
$10,000 & over	32	21	25	10	12
Class Identification					
Propertied class	20	20	34	12	14
Middle class	36	21	24	10	9
Working class	50	24	17	5	4
Occupation					
Professional, business	33	21	22	11	13
White-collar workers	39	20	29	5	7
Farmers	34	24	21	12	9
Blue-collar workers	51	23	18	5	3
Nonlabor	44	19	20	9	8
Union Member					
Yes	52	21	19	5	3
No	40	22	22	8	8
Religion					
Protestant	38	22	22	9	9
Catholic	55	22	17	3	3
Jewish	69	21	7	*	3
City Size					
500,000 & over	55	19	17	4	5
50,000–499,999	43	21	22	8	6
2,500–49,999	31	24	25	10	10
Under 2,500 & rural	36	23	23	10	8

TABLE 1 (*Continued*)

	Compl. Lib.	Pred. Lib.	Middle of Road	Pred. Cons.	Compl. Cons.
Region					
East	54%	18%	19%	5%	4%
South—Goldwater	33	24	16	10	17
South—Johnson	44	23	18	8	7
Midwest	39	23	23	9	6
West	37	22	25	7	9
Grandparents					
None born in U.S.	49	22	19	5	5
Some born in U.S.	35	23	24	9	9
Ethnic Groups					
English	30	21	27	12	10
German	34	20	28	10	8
Scandinavian	39	20	24	10	7
Irish (Catholic)	54	23	18	3	2
Italian	57	19	18	5	1
Eastern or Central European	54	22	15	3	6
Race					
Whites	40	22	22	8	8
Negroes	79	13	7	1	*
Party					
Republican	21	20	30	14	15
Democratic	58	21	16	3	2
Independent	35	24	24	10	7
Ideological Spectrum					
Compl. or pred. lib.	69	21	9	*	1
Middle of road	52	27	17	3	1
Pred. cons.	33	27	29	7	4
Compl. cons.	19	17	28	17	19
Self-Identification					
Lib.	60	21	15	3	1
Middle of road	44	24	23	7	3
Cons.	25	18	27	12	18

* Less than .5%

TABLE 2
GOVERNMENT POWER

	Too Much	About Right	Should Use More	Don't Know
National Totals	26%	36%	31%	7%
Sex				
Male	30	35	29	6
Female	22	37	32	9
Age				
21–29	19	40	36	5
30–49	26	37	31	6
50 & over	29	34	28	9
Education				
Grade school	17	35	33	15
High school	26	39	31	4
College	41	32	25	2
Income				
Under $5,000	20	34	33	13
$5,000–$9,999	27	38	32	3
$10,000 & over	35	40	24	1
Class Identification				
Propertied class	53	30	16	1
Middle class	33	39	25	3
Working class	18	39	34	9
Occupation				
Professional, business	33	39	25	3
White-collar workers	33	37	27	3
Farmers	34	41	18	7
Blue-collar workers	19	36	37	8
Nonlabor	29	31	26	14
Union Member				
Yes	18	40	37	5
No	28	35	29	8
Religion				
Protestant	31	34	27	8
Catholic	13	43	38	6
Jewish	4	47	46	3

TABLE 2 (*Continued*)

	Too Much	About Right	Should Use More	Don't Know
City Size				
500,000 & over	18%	36%	37%	9%
50,000–499,999	21	38	33	8
2,500–49,999	32	39	26	3
Under 2,500 & rural	35	34	24	7
Region				
East	18	35	38	9
South—Goldwater	52	18	18	12
South—Johnson	31	32	28	9
Midwest	22	44	28	6
West	28	37	32	3
Grandparents				
None born in U.S.	18	41	34	7
Some born in U.S.	34	36	25	5
Ethnic Groups				
English	40	35	23	2
German	31	42	24	3
Scandinavian	30	37	30	3
Irish (Catholic)	16	47	34	3
Italian	7	45	43	5
Eastern or Central European	12	44	38	6
Race				
White	29	38	28	5
Negro	2	22	52	24
Party				
Republican	46	32	18	4
Democratic	14	38	38	10
Independent	32	38	26	4
Operational Spectrum				
Compl. lib.	6	41	46	7
Pred. lib.	18	44	33	5
Middle of road	43	34	19	4

TABLE 2 (*Continued*)

	Too Much	About Right	Should Use More	Don't Know
Operational Spectrum (Cont'd.)				
Pred. cons.	65%	24%	6%	5%
Compl. cons.	89	10	*	1
Ideological Spectrum				
Compl. or pred. lib.	3	42	51	4
Middle of road	5	51	40	4
Pred. cons.	33	44	20	3
Compl. cons.	61	22	13	4
Self-Identification				
Lib.	11	41	43	5
Middle of road	23	41	30	6
Cons.	46	28	22	4

* Less than .5%

TABLE 3

IDEOLOGICAL SPECTRUM

	Compl. or Pred. Lib.	Middle of Road	Pred. Cons.	Compl. Cons.
National Totals	16%	34%	20%	30%
Sex				
Male	16	34	18	32
Female	16	34	21	29
Age				
21–29	20	37	21	22
30–49	18	37	19	26
50 & over	13	28	20	39
Education				
Grade school	17	32	21	30
High school	16	36	19	29
College	14	31	19	36

TABLE 3 (*Continued*)

	Compl. or Pred. Lib.	Middle of Road	Pred. Cons.	Compl. Cons.
Income				
Under $5,000	18%	33%	19%	30%
$5,000–$9,999	14	37	21	28
$10,000 & over	18	28	17	37
Class Identification				
Propertied class	4	33	18	45
Middle class	13	32	20	35
Working class	21	35	20	24
Occupation				
Professional, business	19	33	17	31
White-collar workers	17	29	17	37
Farmers	9	28	20	43
Blue-collar workers	18	37	22	23
Nonlabor	10	30	18	42
Union Member				
Yes	21	42	18	19
No	15	31	20	34
Religion				
Protestant	14	28	21	37
Catholic	17	48	18	17
Jewish	44	39	10	7
City Size				
500,000 & over	24	38	17	21
50,000–499,999	12	42	22	24
2,500–49,999	12	32	20	36
Under 2,500 & rural	13	23	20	44
Region				
East	23	39	16	22
South—Goldwater	8	10	25	57
South—Johnson	10	28	20	42
Midwest	16	36	22	26
West	14	38	19	29
Grandparents				
None born in U.S.	18	38	18	26
Some born in U.S.	14	28	22	36

TABLE 3 (*Continued*)

	Compl. or Pred. Lib.	Middle of Road	Pred. Cons.	Compl. Cons.
Race				
White	14%	33%	20%	33%
Negro	42	44	11	3
Party				
Republican	6	22	23	49
Democratic	22	42	17	19
Independent	16	29	20	35
Operational Spectrum				
Compl. lib.	28	43	15	14
Pred. lib.	14	40	23	23
Middle of road	7	28	26	39
Pred. cons.	1	15	19	65
Compl. cons.	2	4	10	84
Self-Identification				
Lib.	28	46	15	11
Middle of road	16	38	22	24
Cons.	7	23	19	51

TABLE 4

SELF-IDENTIFICATION AS LIBERAL OR CONSERVATIVE

	Very Lib.	Mod. Lib.	Middle of Road	Mod. Cons.	Very Cons.	Don't Know
National Totals	6%	20%	34%	24%	6%	10%
Sex						
Male	7	21	33	26	6	7
Female	6	20	35	22	6	11
Age						
21–29	4	22	38	22	4	10
30–49	6	22	36	22	6	8
50 & over	8	18	31	25	8	10

TABLE 4 (*Continued*)

	Very Lib.	Mod. Lib.	Middle of Road	Mod. Cons.	Very Cons.	Don't Know
Education						
Grade school	8%	18%	32%	18%	7%	17%
High school	6	20	38	24	6	6
College	4	26	30	31	5	4
Income						
Under $5,000	8	17	34	20	6	15
$5,000–$9,999	5	23	35	24	7	6
$10,000 & over	5	24	30	32	5	4
Class Identification						
Propertied class	2	16	24	47	10	1
Middle class	5	23	32	30	5	5
Working class	9	19	31	23	8	10
Occupation						
Professional, business	4	24	31	30	6	5
White-collar workers	5	26	34	27	4	4
Farmers	4	19	35	26	5	11
Blue-collar workers	7	19	37	19	6	12
Nonlabor	8	17	32	22	8	13
Union Member						
Yes	8	27	35	17	6	7
No	6	18	34	26	6	10
Religion						
Protestant	6	17	34	25	7	11
Catholic	5	26	38	20	4	7
Jewish	16	45	24	8	2	5
City Size						
500,000 & over	8	23	34	20	5	10
50,000–499,999	7	24	34	21	5	9
2,500–49,999	6	16	33	28	7	10
Under 2,500 & rural	5	16	35	27	8	9
Region						
East	7	25	35	20	5	8
South—Goldwater	5	11	27	30	11	16

TABLE 4 (*Continued*)

	Very Lib.	Mod. Lib.	Middle of Road	Mod. Cons.	Very Cons.	Don't Know
Region (Cont'd.)						
South—Johnson	8%	13%	34%	23%	6%	16%
Midwest	5	22	35	25	6	7
West	6	23	36	24	6	5
Grandparents						
None born in U.S.	6	23	37	22	5	7
Some born in U.S.	5	19	35	26	7	8
Ethnic Groups						
English	6	19	33	31	7	4
German	3	24	36	25	7	5
Scandinavian	7	19	39	27	5	3
Irish (Catholic)	4	31	37	20	4	4
Italian	7	23	43	20	3	4
Eastern or Central European	9	37	35	14	2	3
Race						
White	5	20	36	25	6	8
Negro	17	20	21	11	7	24
Party						
Republican	2	11	31	42	8	6
Democratic	9	26	32	16	6	11
Independent	4	18	43	21	6	8
Operational Spectrum						
Compl. lib.	10	28	35	14	4	9
Pred. lib.	6	21	38	20	6	9
Middle of road	3	17	36	34	6	4
Pred. cons.	3	7	31	44	7	8
Compl. cons.	*	6	15	52	22	5
Ideological Spectrum						
Compl. or pred. lib.	11	36	30	13	3	7
Middle of road	10	29	35	17	6	3
Pred. cons.	5	16	36	31	2	10
Compl. cons.	2	8	25	45	12	8

* Less than .5%

TABLE 5

OPERATIONAL *vs.* IDEOLOGICAL CONCERNS

(The rationale of this table is given on pp. 53 ff. The first column gives the percentage of each group whose average score on Operational Concerns was higher than on Ideological Concerns; the second where the scores were the same; and the third where the score on Ideological Concerns was higher than on Operational.)

	Oper. Higher	Both the Same	Ideol. Higher
National Totals	49%	25%	26%
Sex			
Male	45	27	28
Female	53	23	24
Age			
21–29	50	22	28
30–49	46	29	25
50 & over	52	22	26
Education			
Grade school	59	26	15
High school	47	27	26
College	40	20	40
Income			
Under $5,000	56	25	19
$5,000–$9,999	47	27	26
$10,000 & over	38	21	41
Occupation			
Professional, business	38	24	38
White-collar workers	44	25	31
Farmers	34	29	37
Blue-collar workers	57	26	17
Nonlabor	52	22	26
Religion			
Protestant	46	25	29
Catholic	55	28	17
Jewish	66	21	13
City Size			
500,000 & over	56	25	19
50,000–499,999	50	26	24

TABLE 5 (*Continued*)

	Oper. Higher	Both the Same	Ideol. Higher
City Size (Cont'd.)			
2,500–49,999	43%	22%	35%
Under 2,500 & rural	43	27	30
Region			
East	60	25	15
South—Goldwater	30	25	45
South—Johnson	46	22	32
Midwest	50	25	25
West	40	29	31
Race			
White	46	26	28
Negro	76	21	3
Party			
Republican	34	22	44
Democratic	60	25	15
Independent	42	28	30
Operational Spectrum			
Compl. lib.	69	24	7
Pred. lib.	51	28	21
Middle of road	34	30	36
Pred. cons.	16	15	69
Compl. cons.	6	8	86
Government Power			
Too much	19	20	61
Right amount	56	27	17
Should use more	65	27	8

TABLE 6
INTERNATIONAL PATTERNS

	Compl. Inter.	Pred. Inter.	Mixed	Pred. or Compl. Isol.
National Totals	30%	35%	27%	8%
Sex				
Male	30	36	27	7
Female	30	35	27	8
Age				
21–29	35	36	24	5
30–49	34	36	24	6
50 & over	24	34	31	11
Education				
Grade school	19	34	34	13
High school	30	38	26	6
College	47	30	19	4
Income				
Under $5,000	23	36	29	12
$5,000–$9,999	32	35	27	6
$10,000 & over	45	32	18	5
Occupation				
Professional, business	42	31	23	4
White-collar workers	35	35	24	6
Farmers	25	39	28	8
Blue-collar workers	27	37	27	9
Nonlabor	20	35	32	13
Religion				
Protestant	28	36	27	9
Catholic	38	32	26	4
Jewish	43	37	17	3
City Size				
500,000 & over	33	34	25	8
50,000–499,999	36	33	25	6
2,500–49,999	27	39	27	7
Under 2,500 & rural	24	36	30	10

TABLE 6 (*Continued*)

	Compl. Int.	Pred. Int.	Mixed	Pred. or Compl. Isol.
Region				
East	35%	34%	25%	6%
South—Goldwater	19	33	32	16
South—Johnson	25	39	28	8
Midwest	32	37	25	6
West	30	32	29	9
Grandparents				
None born in U.S.	31	35	26	8
Some born in U.S.	30	35	27	8
Ethnic Groups				
English	33	35	26	6
German	31	38	24	7
Scandinavian	32	36	26	6
Irish (Catholic)	35	32	29	4
Italian	35	35	23	7
Eastern or Central European	42	31	22	5
Race				
White	30	35	27	8
Negro	31	38	27	4
Party				
Republican	28	33	29	10
Democratic	32	35	27	6
Independent	30	38	23	9
Operational Spectrum				
Compl. lib.	35	36	24	5
Pred. lib.	28	37	28	7
Middle of road	29	34	29	8
Pred. cons.	24	35	30	11
Compl. cons.	20	30	31	19
Ideological Spectrum				
Compl. or pred. lib.	41	35	18	6
Middle of road	36	35	26	3
Pred. cons.	24	43	26	7
Compl. cons.	21	31	36	12

TABLE 7

PERSONAL LADDER—AVERAGE RATINGS

	Past	Present	Future	Differences	
				Pres. *vs.* Past	Future *vs.* Pres.
National Totals	5.96	6.85	7.89	+0.89	+1.04
Sex					
Male	5.89	6.76	7.74	+0.87	+0.98
Female	6.02	6.92	8.03	+0.90	+1.11
Age					
21–29	5.08	6.39	8.34	+1.31	+1.95
30–49	5.58	6.82	8.14	+1.24	+1.32
50 & over	6.72	7.04	7.33	+0.32	+0.29
Education					
Grade school	6.03	6.73	7.53	+0.70	+0.80
High school	5.78	6.76	7.96	+0.98	+1.20
College	6.29	7.26	8.24	+0.97	+0.98
Income					
Under $3,000	6.23	6.27	7.06	+0.04	+0.79
$3,000–$4,999	5.72	6.52	7.62	+0.80	+1.10
$5,000–$9,999	5.83	7.03	8.07	+1.20	+1.04
$10,000 & over	6.12	7.41	8.47	+1.29	+1.06
Occupation					
Professional, business	6.19	7.26	8.14	+1.07	+0.88
White-collar workers	5.82	7.03	8.26	+1.21	+1.23
Farmers	6.09	6.78	7.51	+0.69	+0.73
Blue-collar workers	5.46	6.61	8.00	+1.15	+1.39
Nonlabor	7.06	6.88	7.04	−0.18	+0.16
Religion					
Protestant	6.05	6.88	7.86	+0.83	+0.98
Catholic	5.71	6.83	8.04	+1.12	+1.21
Jewish	6.16	7.26	8.14	+1.10	+0.88
City Size					
500,000 & over	5.76	6.65	7.96	+0.89	+1.31
50,000–499,999	5.83	6.82	8.05	+0.99	+1.23
2,500–49,999	6.30	7.03	7.91	+0.73	+0.88
Under 2,500 & rural	6.11	7.01	7.69	+0.90	+0.68

TABLE 7 (*Continued*)

	Past	Present	Future	Pres. vs. Past	Future vs. Pres.
Region					
East	5.87	6.92	7.96	+1.05	+1.04
South—Goldwater	5.78	6.52	7.48	+0.74	+0.96
South—Johnson	6.26	6.77	7.91	+0.51	+1.14
Midwest	6.07	6.95	7.97	+0.88	+1.02
West	5.65	6.78	7.85	+1.13	+1.07
Grandparents					
None born in U.S.	6.03	6.98	7.89	+0.95	+0.91
Some born in U.S.	5.92	6.79	7.89	+0.87	+1.10
Race					
White	6.06	6.96	7.92	+0.90	+0.96
Negro	5.11	5.84	7.72	+0.73	+1.88
Party					
Republican	6.37	7.20	7.83	+0.83	+0.63
Democratic	5.81	6.67	7.90	+0.86	+1.23
Independent	5.86	6.88	7.96	+1.02	+1.08
Operational Spectrum					
Compl. lib.	5.67	6.62	7.88	+0.95	+1.26
Pred. lib.	5.86	6.95	7.94	+1.09	+0.99
Middle of road	5.98	6.90	7.81	+0.92	+0.91
Pred. cons.	6.49	7.28	8.11	+0.79	+0.83
Compl. cons.	7.21	7.70	8.11	+0.49	+0.41
Government Power					
Too much	6.46	7.25	7.96	+0.79	+0.71
About right amount	5.85	6.86	7.90	+1.01	+1.04
Should use more	5.64	6.63	7.91	+0.99	+1.28
Ideological Spectrum					
Compl. or pred. lib.	5.54	6.50	7.81	+0.96	+1.31
Middle of road	5.77	6.74	7.92	+0.97	+1.18
Pred. cons.	5.69	6.99	8.00	+1.30	+1.01
Compl. cons.	6.56	7.20	7.83	+0.64	+0.63

TABLE 8
NATIONAL LADDER—AVERAGE RATINGS

	Past	Present	Future	Differences	
				Pres. vs. Past	Future vs. Pres.
National Totals	6.12	6.50	7.68	+0.38	+1.18
Sex					
Male	6.23	6.68	7.74	+0.45	+1.06
Female	6.03	6.33	7.62	+0.30	+1.29
Age					
21–29	5.91	6.33	7.46	+0.42	+1.13
30–49	5.99	6.54	7.81	+0.55	+1.27
50 & over	6.36	6.50	7.57	+0.14	+1.07
Education					
Grade school	6.12	6.81	8.06	+0.69	+1.25
High school	6.14	6.44	7.69	+0.30	+1.25
College	6.12	6.14	7.04	+0.02	+0.90
Income					
Under $3,000	5.98	6.31	7.81	+0.33	+1.50
$3,000–$4,999	6.15	6.63	7.79	+0.48	+1.16
$5,000–$9,999	6.06	6.51	7.65	+0.45	+1.14
$10,000 & over	6.39	6.50	7.47	+0.11	+0.97
Occupation					
Professional, business	6.22	6.35	7.37	+0.13	+1.02
White-collar workers	6.10	6.43	7.64	+0.33	+1.21
Farmers	6.68	6.40	6.93	−0.28	+0.53
Blue-collar workers	5.92	6.59	7.98	+0.67	+1.39
Nonlabor	6.34	6.53	7.58	+0.19	+1.05
Religion					
Protestant	6.26	6.35	7.50	+0.09	+1.15
Catholic	5.98	6.87	8.15	+0.89	+1.28
Jewish	5.09	6.78	7.72	+1.69	+0.94
City Size					
500,000 & over	5.85	6.63	7.92	+0.78	+1.29
50,000–499,999	6.05	6.07	7.90	+0.02	+1.23
2,500–49,999	6.36	6.39	7.74	+0.03	+1.35
Under 2,500 & rural	6.38	6.26	7.16	−0.12	+0.90

TABLE 8 (*Continued*)

	Past	Present	Future	Differences Pres. *vs.* Past	Future *vs.* Pres.
Region					
East	6.01	6.84	8.07	+0.83	+1.23
South—Goldwater	6.24	5.81	6.53	−0.43	+0.72
South—Johnson	6.21	6.46	7.75	+0.25	+1.29
Midwest	6.22	6.49	7.61	+0.27	+1.12
West	5.99	6.30	7.55	+0.31	+1.25
Grandparents					
None born in U.S.	6.26	6.94	7.88	+0.68	+0.94
Some born in U.S.	6.07	6.31	7.58	+0.24	+1.27
Race					
White	6.26	6.48	7.53	+0.22	+1.05
Negro	4.89	6.62	8.97	+1.73	+2.35
Party					
Republican	6.83	6.07	6.98	−0.76	+0.91
Democratic	5.75	6.89	8.29	+1.14	+1.40
Independent	6.12	6.08	7.06	−0.04	+0.98
Operational Spectrum					
Compl. lib.	5.87	6.96	8.31	+1.09	+1.35
Pred. lib.	6.13	6.62	7.85	+0.49	+1.23
Middle of road	6.32	6.18	7.12	−0.14	+0.94
Pred. cons.	6.55	5.86	6.67	−0.69	+0.81
Compl. cons.	6.31	5.12	5.54	−1.19	+0.42
Government Power					
Too much	6.47	5.58	6.43	−0.89	+0.85
About right amount	6.20	6.89	8.02	+0.69	+1.13
Should use more	5.76	6.72	8.20	+0.96	+1.48
Ideological Spectrum					
Compl. or pred. lib.	5.59	6.83	8.06	+1.24	+1.23
Middle of road	5.94	6.93	8.30	+0.99	+1.37
Pred. cons.	6.18	6.33	7.56	+0.15	+1.23
Compl. cons.	6.59	5.86	6.64	−0.73	+0.78

TABLE 8 (*Continued*)

	Past	Present	Future	Differences Pres. *vs.* Past	Differences Future *vs.* Pres.
Self-Identification					
Lib.	5.80	6.83	8.25	+1.03	+1.42
Middle of road	6.10	6.52	7.70	+0.42	+1.18
Cons.	6.44	6.15	7.12	−0.29	+0.97
International Patterns					
Compl. inter.	6.10	6.72	7.98	+0.62	+1.26
Pred. inter.	6.23	6.53	7.81	+0.30	+1.28
Mixed	6.10	6.35	7.41	+0.25	+1.06
Compl. or pred. isol.	5.93	5.86	6.17	−0.07	+0.31

TABLE 9

PARTY IDENTIFICATIONS

	Repub- lican	Demo- cratic	Inde- pendent	Other or Don't Know
National Totals	24%	49%	24%	3%
Sex				
Male	23	49	26	2
Female	25	50	22	3
Age				
21–29	19	47	31	3
30–49	20	52	25	3
50 & over	31	48	19	2
Education				
Grade school	20	58	18	4
High school	22	50	26	2
College	38	34	26	2
Income				
Under $5,000	21	55	21	3
$5,000–$9,999	22	50	26	2
$10,000 & over	39	34	25	2

TABLE 9 (*Continued*)

	Repub-lican	Demo-cratic	Inde-pendent	Other or Don't Know
Class Identification				
Propertied	54%	22%	23%	1%
Middle	33	38	26	3
Working	16	62	21	1
Occupation				
Professional, business	34	37	26	3
White-collar workers	25	45	29	1
Farmers	28	44	28	*
Blue-collar workers	17	57	24	2
Nonlabor	29	51	16	4
Union Member				
Yes	15	60	23	2
No	27	46	24	3
Religion				
Protestant	29	45	24	2
Catholic	12	63	22	3
Jewish	9	65	22	4
City Size				
500,000 & over	20	54	23	3
50,000–499,999	20	56	22	2
2,500–49,999	33	41	23	3
Under 2,500 & rural	28	44	26	2
Region				
East	26	53	18	3
South—Goldwater	18	57	21	4
South—Johnson	15	56	25	4
Midwest	29	42	28	1
West	27	46	26	1
Grandparents				
None born in U.S.	22	52	24	2
Some born in U.S.	29	42	27	2
Ethnic Groups				
English	35	36	27	2
German	33	38	28	1

TABLE 9 (*Continued*)

	Repub-lican	Demo-cratic	Inde-pendent	Other or Don't Know
Ethnic Groups (Cont'd.)				
Scandinavian	31%	37%	30%	2%
Irish (Catholic)	14	59	26	1
Italian	14	63	22	1
Eastern or Central				
European	15	63	20	2
Race				
White	27	45	26	2
Negro	3	87	6	4
Operational Spectrum				
Compl. lib.	12	66	19	3
Pred. lib.	23	49	26	2
Middle of road	36	36	27	1
Pred. cons.	46	19	33	2
Compl. cons.	56	16	26	2
Government Power				
Too much	43	26	29	2
About right amount	21	53	25	1
Should use more	15	62	20	3
Ideological Spectrum				
Compl. or pred. lib.	8	66	25	1
Middle of road	16	60	21	3
Pred. cons.	30	42	25	3
Compl. cons.	40	30	28	2
Self-identification				
Lib.	12	66	20	2
Middle of road	22	47	29	2
Cons.	41	37	21	1
International Patterns				
Compl. inter.	24	51	24	1
Pred. inter.	23	49	26	2
Mixed	28	49	21	2
Compl. or pred. isol.	32	36	28	4

* Less than .5%

Notes

1. For background reading in American political theory, see *The Growth of American Thought* by Merle Curti (New York: Harper and Row, 1964); *The American Mind: An Interpretation of American Thought and Character since the 1880's* by Henry Steele Commager (New Haven: Yale University Press, 1950); *The American Enlightenment* by Adrienne Koch (New York: George Braziller, 1965); *The Liberal Tradition in America* by Louis Hartz (New York: Harcourt, Brace and World, 1955); *The Conservative Mind* by Russell Kirk (Chicago: Henry Regnery Co., A Gateway Edition, 1960); and *Conservatism Revisited* by Peter Viereck (New York: Charles Scribner's Sons, 1949). Excellent short synopses will be found in *History of Political Theory* by Benoit-Snullyan (Boston: Student Outlines Co., 1938) and several articles in *Collier's Encyclopedia*.

2. On this point, the chapter on the "New Deal" in *The Liberal Tradition in America* is relevant (Note 1 above).

3. *Washington Post,* April 25, 1966.

4. For an extended discussion of this subject, including Richard Center's pioneering work in this field, see *The American Voter* by Campbell, Converse, Miller, and Stokes (New York: John Wiley and Sons, 1960), pp. 341 ff. Earlier, Lazarsfeld, Berelson, and Gaudet had found subjective class identifications more important in determining voting behavior than occupation: *The People's Choice* (New York: Columbia University Press, 1944), p. 20.

5. *The American Mind* (Note 1 above), p. 336.

6. Commager, in alluding to the pragmatic cast of American

thought as a historical trait, had this to say in *The American Mind* (Note 1 above), page 8: "Theories and speculations disturbed the American, and he avoided abstruse philosophies of government or conduct. . . . In politics, too, he profoundly mistrusted the abstract and the doctrinaire."

7. *The American People and China* by A. T. Steele (New York: McGraw-Hill, 1966).

8. Contrary to our findings in this respect, Berelson, Lazarsfeld, and McPhee found no correlation between domestic issues and international issues in 1948 (*Voting: A Study of Opinion Formation in a Presidential Campaign*—Chicago: University of Chicago Press, 1954, p. 197); and Campbell *et al.* found none in 1956 (*The American Voter*, Note 4 above), p. 197.

9. *New York Times Magazine*, February 28, 1965.

10. For a study of this subject, conducted in mid-1964 by the Survey Research Center of the University of Michigan, see *The American People and China* (Note 7 above).

11. The Self-Anchoring Striving Scale was developed by Hadley Cantril with the assistance of Franklin P. Kilpatrick. A full description of the technique is given in Cantril's *The Pattern of Human Concerns* (New Brunswick, N.J.: Rutgers University Press, 1965), which also reports and analyzes results obtained when the device was used on samples of national populations whose numbers total about 30% of the world's population, including a study of the United States in 1959.

12. The code used is described in *The Pattern of Human Concerns* (Note 11 above).

13. See *The Pattern of Human Concerns* (Note 11 above), p. 43.

14. As the matter was put on page 135 of *The American Voter* (Note 4 above): "We know that persons who identify with one of the parties typically have held the same partisan tie for all or almost all of their adult lives."

15. Campbell *et al.* review their findings in this connection on page 147 of *The American Voter* (Note 4 above).

16. "The American Catholic is Changing" by John Leo, for-

merly associate editor of *Commonweal,* writing in the *New York Times Sunday Magazine,* November 14, 1965.

17. Our own figures show this, but for results based on large cumulative samples, see the Gallup Poll release of December 13, 1964.

18. As the late V. O. Key, Jr., pointed out well in advance of the 1964 election, a minority party to be "serviceable" must clearly not threaten basic policies that have won majority acceptance (*The Responsible Electorate*—Cambridge: Harvard University Press, 1966).

19. D. J. Boorstin (ed.), *An American Primer* (University of Chicago Press, 1966), Vol. I, p. 3.

20. S. E. Morrison, "The Mayflower Compact," in *An American Primer,* Vol. I, p. 5. (See Note 19.)

21. H. S. Commager, "The Declaration of Independence," in *An American Primer,* Vol. I, p. 73. (See Note 19.)

22. D. Malone, "Jefferson's First Inaugural Address," in *An American Primer,* Vol. I, p. 217. (See Note 19.)

23. D. Malone, "Jefferson's First Inaugural Address," in *An American Primer,* Vol. I, p. 218. (See Note 19.)

About the Authors

Since 1955 Lloyd A. Free and Hadley Cantril have been Director and Chairman of the Board, respectively, of the Institute for International Social Research of Princeton, New Jersey. The Institute has done public opinion research in some twenty-one countries, taking sample polls representing about one third of the world's population.

In his private capacity, Mr. Free has conducted a great many political polls in recent times, both in connection with gubernatorial elections and Presidential primaries, and in his early years managed several successful Congressional campaigns. Formerly, he worked for the BBC and CBS; was a Lecturer in the School of Public and International Affairs at Princeton University; twice served as Editor of *The Public Opinion Quarterly;* and headed the State Department's world-wide information program which later became USIA. He subsequently served as a consultant to President Eisenhower and co-chaired a special task force to advise President Kennedy.

Dr. Cantril, who has an international reputation as a social psychologist, has authored, co-authored, or edited some seventeen other books in his field and contributed over a hundred articles to scholarly journals. A pioneer in the field of public opinion research, he was formerly Director of the Office of Public Opinion Research of Princeton University. He has been advisor in the field of social psychology to all but one of the past five Administrations. He is Research Associate of the Department of Psychology at Princeton University, of which he was formerly Chairman.